AT RISK IN THE PROMISED LAND

A Commentary on the Book of

JUDGES

E. JOHN HAMLIN

WILLIAM B. EERDMANS PUBLISHING CO., GRAND RAPIDS

THE HANDSEL PRESS, LTD, EDINBURGH

Copyright © 1990 by Wm. B. Eerdmans Publishing Company
First published 1990 by Wm. B. Eerdmans Publishing Company,
255 Jefferson Ave. S.E., Grand Rapids, Mich. 49503
and
The Handsel Press Limited
53 Montgomery Street, Edinburgh EH7 5JX

Printed in the United States of America

Library of Congress Cataloging in Publication Data

Hamlin, E. John
At risk in the Promised Land: a commentary on the book of Judges /
E. John Hamlin.
p.   cm. — (International theological commentary)
Includes bibliographical references.
ISBN 0-8028-0432-2
1. Bible. O.T. Judges—Commentaries.   I. Title.   II. Series.
BS1305.3.H36   1990
222′.3207—dc20   90-35786
                                                                      CIP

British Library Cataloguing in Publication Data

Hamlin, E. John
At risk in the Promised Land.
1. Bible. O.T. Judges—Critical studies
I. Title   II. Series
222.3206
ISBN 1-871828-03-1

Unless otherwise noted, the Scripture quotations in this publication are from the
Revised Standard Version of the Bible, copyrighted 1946, 1952 © 1971, 1973 by
the Division of Christian Education of the National Council of Churches of Christ
in the U.S.A., and used by permission.

CONTENTS

ABBREVIATIONS

IB	*Interpreter's Bible*
IDB	*Interpreter's Dictionary of the Bible*
JB	Jerusalem Bible
KJV	King James (or Authorized) Version
LXX	Septuagint
mg	margin
NAB	New American Bible
NEB	New English Bible
NIV	New International Version
NT	New Testament
OT	Old Testament
RSV	Revised Standard Version
TDNT	*Theological Dictionary of the New Testament*
TDOT	*Theological Dictionary of the Old Testament*
TEV	Today's English Version

EDITORS' PREFACE

The Old Testament alive in the Church: this is the goal of the
International Theological Commentary. Arising out of changing,
unsettled times, this Scripture speaks with an authentic voice to our
own troubled world. It witnesses to God's ongoing purpose and
to his caring presence in the universe without ignoring those
experiences of life that cause one to question his existence and love.
This commentary series is written by front-rank scholars who
treasure the life of faith.

Addressed to ministers and Christian educators, the *International Theological Commentary* moves beyond the usual critical-
historical approach to the Bible and offers a *theological* interpretation of the Hebrew text. Thus, engaging larger textual units of
the biblical writings, the authors of these volumes assist the reader
in the appreciation of the theology underlying the text as well as
its place in the thought of the Hebrew Scriptures. But more, since
the Bible is the book of the believing community, its text has
acquired ever more meaning through an ongoing interpretation.
This growth of interpretation may be found both within the Bible
itself and in the continuing scholarship of the Church.

Contributors to the *International Theological Commentary* are
Christians—persons who affirm the witness of the New Testament
concerning Jesus Christ. For Christians, the Bible is *one* scripture
containing the Old and New Testaments. For this reason, a
commentary on the Old Testament may not ignore the second
part of the canon, namely, the New Testament.

Since its beginning, the Church has recognized a special relationship between the two Testaments. But the precise character
of this bond has been difficult to define. Thousands of books and
articles have discussed the issue. The diversity of views represented

in these publications makes us aware that the Church is not of one mind in expressing the "how" of this relationship. The authors of this commentary share a developing consensus that any serious explanation of the Old Testament's relationship to the New will uphold the integrity of the Old Testament. Even though Christianity is rooted in the soil of the Hebrew Scriptures, the biblical interpreter must take care lest he "christianize" these Scriptures.

Authors writing in this commentary will, no doubt, hold varied views concerning *how* the Old Testament relates to the New. No attempt has been made to dictate one viewpoint in this matter. With the whole Church, we are convinced that the relationship between the two Testaments is real and substantial. But we recognize also the diversity of opinions among Christian scholars when they attempt to articulate fully the nature of this relationship.

In addition to the Christian Church, there exists another people for whom the Old Testament is important, namely, the Jewish community. Both Jews and Christians claim the Hebrew Bible as Scripture. Jews believe that the basic teachings of this Scripture point toward, and are developed by, the Talmud, which assumed its present form about A.D. 500. On the other hand, Christians hold that the Old Testament finds its fulfillment in the New Testament. The Hebrew Bible, therefore, belongs to both the Church and the Synagogue.

Recent studies have demonstrated how profoundly early Christianity reflects a Jewish character. This fact is not surprising because the Christian movement arose out of the context of first-century Judaism. Further, Jesus himself was Jewish, as were the first Christians. It is to be expected, therefore, that Jewish and Christian interpretations of the Hebrew Bible will reveal similarities *and* disparities. Such is the case. The authors of the *International Theological Commentary* will refer to the various Jewish traditions that they consider important for an appreciation of the Old Testament text. Such references will enrich our understanding of certain biblical passages and, as an extra gift, offer us insight into the relationship of Judaism to early Christianity.

An important second aspect of the present series is its *international* character. In the past, Western church leaders were considered to be *the* leaders of the Church—at least by those living in the West! The theology and biblical exegesis done by these scholars dominated the thinking of the Church. Most commentaries were produced in the Western world and reflected the lifestyle, needs, and thoughts of its civilization. But the Christian Church is a worldwide community. People who belong to this universal Church reflect differing thoughts, needs, and lifestyles.

Today the fastest growing churches in the world are to be found, not in the West, but in Africa, Indonesia, South America, Korea, Taiwan, and elsewhere. By the end of this century, Christians in these areas will outnumber those who live in the West. In our age, especially, a commentary on the Bible must transcend the parochialism of Western civilization and be sensitive to issues that are the special problems of persons who live outside of the "Christian" West, issues such as race relations, personal survival and fulfillment, liberation, revolution, famine, tyranny, disease, war, the poor, religion and state. Inspired of God, the authors of the Old Testament knew what life is like on the edge of existence. They addressed themselves to everyday people who often faced more than everyday problems. Refusing to limit God to the "spiritual," they portrayed him as one who heard and knew the cries of people in pain (see Exod. 3:7-8). The contributors to the *International Theological Commentary* are persons who prize the writings of these biblical authors as a word of life to our world today. They read the Hebrew Scriptures in the twin contexts of ancient Israel and our modern day.

The scholars selected as contributors underscore the international aspect of the series. Representing very different geographical, ideological, and ecclesiastical backgrounds, they come from more than seventeen countries. Besides scholars from such traditional countries as England, Scotland, France, Italy, Switzerland, Canada, New Zealand, Australia, South Africa, and the United States, contributors from the following places are included: Israel, Indonesia, India, Thailand, Singapore, Taiwan, and countries of Eastern Europe. Such diversity makes for richness of thought. Christian scholars living in Buddhist, Muslim, or Socialist lands may be able to offer the World Church insights into the biblical message—insights to which the scholarship of the West could be blind.

The proclamation of the biblical message is the focal concern of the *International Theological Commentary*. Generally speaking, the authors of these commentaries value the historical-critical studies of past scholars, but they are convinced that these studies by themselves are not enough. The Bible is more than an object of critical study; it is the revelation of God. In the written Word, God has disclosed himself and his will to humankind. Our authors see themselves as servants of the Word which, when rightly received, brings *shalom* to both the individual and the community.

—GEORGE A. F. KNIGHT
— FREDRICK CARLSON HOLMGREN

AUTHOR'S PREFACE

Ideas for this book were first formed from lectures given at Thailand Theological Seminary, now the McGilvary Faculty of Theology of Payap University, Chiang Mai, Thailand; Trinity Theological Seminary, Singapore; and in Rangoon, Burma, as a faculty member of the Southeast Asia Graduate School of Theology. I wish to express appreciation to Trinity Lutheran Theological Seminary in Columbus, Ohio, for the use of their fine library facilities and to Union Theological Seminary, New York City, for a three month residency while working on one segment of Judges.

Former colleagues in Thailand, Herbert Grether and Kosuke Koyama, read major sections of the manuscript and made useful suggestions. Friends at Bristol Village, Waverly, Ohio, including Mildred Glenn and William Paddock, also gave their reactions to parts of the manuscript. Series editors Fredrick Holmgren and George Knight gave careful attention to the entire manuscript. Finally, my wife Frances Jane Cade Hamlin was critic, proofreader, gentle helper, and loving companion from beginning to end.

—E. JOHN HAMLIN

INTRODUCTION

OUR PROMISED LAND

A proper understanding of the meaning of the land will help readers see the contemporary relevance of the book of Judges. In Christian symbolism, the land of Canaan has come to be a code word for heaven, and the Promised Land a haven waiting for us after the trials of life are over. In the Hebrew Scriptures, however, the Promised Land is a very concrete *space* for living in freedom and *place* for living in security. It is promised to the patriarchs and given to Israel under Joshua, who, after dethroning the powers in Canaan (Josh. 6–12), establishes a new society to preserve living space and place for the people (chs. 13–22; cf. E. John Hamlin, *Inheriting the Land: A Commentary on the Book of Joshua,* parts II and III). The Promised Land in Judges is neither heaven nor haven. It is the God-given arena where the gifts of freedom (space) and security (place) are constantly threatened both from without and from within and are preserved or lost by real people. God is seen to be present behind the scenes as Judge and Savior.

Contemporary readers should see the Promised Land as the living space and place given them by God in Thailand, the Philippines, Singapore, Burma, China, or wherever they live. They will see their particular arena of freedom and security (whether threatened or preserved) as part of the living space (under the heavens) and place (the earth) given to all the human family by the Creator, in which each member of the family has a right to its own space and place. We may learn from Judges about the threats to and preservation of our own and others' living space and place— in short, about the risks of life in our Promised Land.

1

JUDGES IN CONTEXT

The seemingly inconsequential words "Now . . . it came to pass . . ." at the beginning of the book of Judges (Judg. 1:1 KJV) carry an important theological message. They tell us that the ultimate context for the study of the book of Judges is the entire panorama which begins with creation, and extends on to Abraham, Moses, Joshua, the Judges, Samuel, David, the kings of Israel, and Jesus Christ.

"Now it came to pass . . ." is a translation of a Hebrew phrase which always signifies a continuation of a previous narrative. The same is true of the single words "now" or "and" at the beginning of a section of narrative (see note below, p. 3). Thus the book of Judges begins as a sequel to the story of Joshua, where the same words (Josh. 1:1 KJV) make that account a continuation of the narrative in the book of Deuteronomy. The chain continues on back to Numbers, Leviticus, Exodus, and the story of Abraham (Deut. 1:3 KJV; Num. 1:1 KJV; Lev. 1:1 KJV; Exod. 1:1 KJV; Gen. 12:1). Not until we go back to the opening words of Genesis do we find the real beginning of the continued story: "In the beginning God created the heavens and the earth" (1:1). All that follows is sequel.

The book of Ruth continues the narrative following Judges and is succeeded by 1–2 Samuel and 1–2 Kings (Ruth 1:1; 1 Sam. 1:1; 2 Sam. 1:1; 1 Kgs. 1:1; 2 Kgs. 1:1, all KJV). The books of Ezra and Nehemiah extend the continued story beyond the fall of Jerusalem to its restoration (Ezra 1:1; Neh. 1:1 KJV).

When we open the New Testament we find in the Gospel of Matthew the same literary device. There it is the Greek particle *de* which "serves to mark a transition to something new" (J. H. Thayer, *A Greek-English Lexicon of the New Testament* [1956; repr. Peabody, Mass.: Hendrickson, 1981], 125): "*Now* the birth of Jesus Christ took place in this way. . . . *Now* when Jesus was born in Bethlehem . . ." (Matt. 1:18; 2:1). It appears that the Gospel writer was interpreting the new era of Jesus Christ in relation to the narrative histories of the Old Testament, as their continuation and fulfillment.

Of course this does not mean that the author of the book of Judges knew all that was to happen, or even the whole record of what went before, as we now have it. However, if we are right in locating the author in the days after the death of King Josiah (609 B.C.E.; see below, p. 4), we may assume that he knew about the patriarchs, the Exodus and wilderness wanderings, the settlement on the land, the rise and fall of the monarchy, as well as the teaching of the prophets of the 8th and 7th cents. The editors of the canon of the Hebrew Scriptures and the New Testament, who carefully placed these connecting phrases at the beginning of each book, saw the continuity of the whole story, and we as present-day readers have the same advantage.

Reading Judges with this context in mind will help us to look for connections with other parts of the Bible, whether or not these were intended by the author. For example, the book of Judges gives us a clue to a better understanding of the history of Israel under the monarchy. The author's view of the kingship is related to the rise of David, and from NT perspective we can see a relationship to the coming of the greater Son of David, Jesus Christ. Readers will note the similarity between the two annunciation stories in Judg. 13 and Luke 1. Some of these connections are suggested in "perspectives" which follow each section below.

Note on the Hebrew Expression way-yehi

The KJV preserves the literal meaning of the Hebrew expression *wayyehi*, "Now it came to pass." This sounds awkward in present-day English and has been dropped in modern translations. The Hebrew phrase is composed of the conjunction *waw*, which may be translated as "and," "then," or "now," used in a temporal sense to indicate a continuation of the preceding narrative. This word is often used by itself. The second part, *yehi*, may be translated as "it came to pass," "it happened that," or "there was," again as a further development of what has taken place in the previous narrative.

THE AUTHOR OF JUDGES

Judges is part of the Deuteronomic history of Israel (Deuteronomy–2 Kings) which dates from the late 7th and early 6th cents. B.C.E., though some parts of it were added after the fall of Jerusalem (e.g., 2 Kgs. 25:27-30). Many scholars believe that this is the work of a *single* author or editor, while others see it as the product of a *group* or school of writers who shared the point of view of the book of Deuteronomy. The book of Judges shows evidence of careful composition by an individual member of this group, with a particular point of view and purpose in mind. Although there is no hard evidence to date the book of Judges, the following hypothesis seems likely.

Unlike the author of the book of Joshua in the hopeful early years of the reign of Josiah, the author of Judges (we will call him the "Scribe"; see note below) most likely composed his work in the time *after the death of Josiah* when the "false pen of the scribes" had brought Covenant teaching into disrepute (Jer. 8:8), when chaos was threatening the nation from two directions: (1) the unfaithfulness of both leaders and people (cf. Judg. 2:11-13), and (2) the attacks of external enemies (cf. 2:14-15). The book of Judges seems to fit the time of King Jehoiakim and the prophet Jeremiah, *about five hundred years after the events recounted in the book of Judges itself* (12th-11th cents.; see historical outline below, pp. 6-8).

Note on the Office of the Scribe in Ancient Israel

Although the office of royal scribe dates back to the time of David and Solomon (cf. 2 Sam. 8:17; 20:25; 1 Kgs. 4:3), the scribes became especially prominent beginning with the reign of Josiah (640 B.C.E.). This has been called "an age of scribes" (James Muilenburg, "Baruch the Scribe," in *Proclamation and Presence,* ed. John I. Durham and J. Roy Porter [Richmond: John Knox and London: SCM, 1970], 217-18). Four scribes (RSV "secretaries") during that time were Shaphan (2 Kgs. 22:3, 12), Elishama (Jer. 36:12, 20-21), Jeremiah's secretary Baruch (36:26), and Jonathan (37:15, 20). The family of Shaphan the scribe was important in the history of the period. His son Ahikam was a participant in the events leading to the discovery of the Book of the Covenant, which included much of the present book of Deuteronomy (2 Kgs. 22:12, 14), and intervened to save Jeremiah's life from the princes (Jer. 26:24). The house of another son, Gemariah, was the place where Baruch read Jeremiah's scroll "in the hearing of all the people" (Jer. 36:10), and Gemariah urged King Jehoiakim not to burn the scroll (v. 25). A third son, Elasah, carried Jeremiah's letter to the exiles in Babylon some time after 597 (Jer. 29:3). Shaphan's grandson, Gedaliah son of Ahikam, took care of Jeremiah after the fall of Jerusalem (Jer. 39:14). He was appointed governor of Judah by the Babylonians (Jer. 40:11) and urged the people not to be afraid of their conquerors (v. 9). Another grandson, Micaiah the son of Gemariah, reported the contents of Jeremiah's scroll to the princes (Jer. 36:11-13).

Court scribes may have been responsible for much literary activity of the late 7th cent. and later (John L. McKenzie, "Reflections on Wisdom," *Journal of Biblical Literature* 86 [1967]: 8; Moshe Weinfeld, "Deuteronomy: The Present State of Inquiry," *Journal of Biblical Literature* 86 [1967]: 249-62, esp. 254). It was these scribes, says James Muilenburg, who "were not only copyists, but also and more particularly composers who gave to their works their form and structure, and determined to a considerable degree their wording and terminology." He suggests that the authors of the Deuteronomic history might have been members of the scribal family of Shaphan ("Baruch the Scribe," 219-20). The author of Judges may well have been one of them.

HISTORY INTENTIONALLY REMEMBERED

I would like to compare the book of Judges with the Chinese historical novel, *The Three Kingdoms,* which is well known not only in China, but in Southeast Asia as well.

1. Like Judges, *The Three Kingdoms* (Chinese *San Guo,* Thai *Sam Kok*) was written in its final form long after the events which it describes. Luo Guan-zhong based his 14th cent. C.E. novel on traditions of events which occurred over a thousand years earlier, in the 2nd and 3rd cents. The author of Judges wrote in the latter part of the 7th cent. B.C.E. about events which took place in the 12th cent.

2. Like Judges, *The Three Kingdoms* is about heroes and villains of the past. The clever Zhuge Liang may be compared with Ehud, the courageous Guan Yu with Deborah, the good ruler Liu Bei with Gideon or Jephthah, while the wicked Cao Cao reminds us of Abimelech.

3. Like the author of Judges, Luo Guan-zhong wrote with a particular intention; he was not just giving information. In recalling the times of cruelty by the powerful, suffering of the common

people, contests for power among ruling classes, and fierce struggles motivated by self-interest, he was pleading with the people of his own and later generations for benevolent rule, loyalty, and bold imagination and for resolute opposition to despotism (Chen Min-sheng, "On The Three Kingdoms," 127-28). Similarly, the author of Judges was not merely passing on information about the period before the Monarchy. He wrote as a theological interpreter of the past with a message for his contemporaries as well as for readers of later ages, including our own. The task of a commentary like this is to uncover that message.

A PROPOSED HISTORICAL CONTEXT OF THE BOOK OF JUDGES

Although many uncertainties make a reconstruction of the history of Israel difficult, the following summary will give the reader of this commentary some historical perspective for a better understanding of the book.

About 1200 B.C.E.

A group of escaped slaves under Joshua enters Canaan (Josh. 1–12). Oppressed Canaanites like Rahab's family (Josh. 2:8-21; 6:25) and the Gibeonites (Josh. 9), stimulated by the possibilities of liberation, assist in the overthrow of the Canaanite ruling powers, and many join with the Israelites as a new society is set up in Canaan (Josh. 13–22).

1150-1000 B.C.E.

The events described in the book of Judges take place after Joshua's death.

1000-922 B.C.E.

Samuel, Saul, David, and Solomon succeed in establishing a monarchy (1–2 Samuel; 1 Kgs. 1–11). David is later held to have been the ideal king. Traditions about the judge-saviors of the period before the Monarchy are handed down.

922-722 B.C.E.

The period of the two kingdoms: Israel in the north and Judah in the south (1 Kgs. 12–2 Kgs. 16). Assyria brings the northern kingdom to an end and carries the northern tribes into exile (2 Kgs. 17:1-6; 18:9-11). During this period the prophets Amos and Hosea are active in the north. Micah and Isaiah are active in Judah.

722-587 B.C.E.

The kingdom of Judah alone of all the tribes survives (2 Kgs. 17:18). *Hezekiah* (715-687) carries out a religious reform (2 Kgs. 18:1-7) in the time of the prophet Isaiah. His son Manasseh (687-642) turns away from his father's reforms (2 Kgs. 21:1-18). Isaiah is active in this period.

During this time a group of reforming priests and teachers gather the Moses traditions together into what is now most of Deuteronomy. One of this group writes a new edition of the story of Joshua as a model for the young King *Josiah*. Josiah turns to the LORD away from the corruptions of his royal grandfather Manasseh, to carry out a great reform movement in 622 inspired by the discovery of a book of the law in the temple (2 Kgs. 22:3-20; 23:1-22; the book referred to was probably the main part of Deuteronomy).

After the death of Josiah in 609 in a battle with Egypt (2 Kgs. 23:29-30), Egyptian imperial power places Josiah's son *Jehoiakim* (609-598) on the throne as a puppet king (2 Kgs. 23:34-36). As we learn from Jeremiah (Jer. 7:5-11; 22:13-17; 23:9-14), this is a time of great idolatry, immorality, and injustice. Jehoiakim's son *Jehoiachin,* along with many of the ruling elite and leading citizens, is carried into exile (2 Kgs. 24:10-16).

Judah's last king, *Zedekiah,* is captured by Babylonian forces in 587 (2 Kgs. 25:6-7), Jerusalem is destroyed, and a large number of citizens are taken into exile (2 Kgs. 25:8-17). The prophets Jeremiah, Zephaniah, and Habakkuk are active during this period. Ezekiel is taken into exile in 597 (Ezek. 1:1), and Jeremiah is taken to Egypt after 587 (Jer. 43:5-7).

A reform group of historian-theologians writes a history of Israel called the Deuteronomic history (Deuteronomy–2 Kings). A member of this group, whom we call the Scribe, gathers traditions about the heroes of the period before the Monarchy and incorporates them in the book of Judges.

PART I
THE PROLOGUE:
AFTER JOSHUA

Judges 1:1–2:5

SETTING THE STAGE
Judges 1:1

"THE PEOPLE OF ISRAEL"

The major theme of the entire book of Judges is "the people of Israel" (Heb. *bene yisrael;* KJV "children of Israel"; NEB "Israelites"). Therefore it is important for the present-day reader to understand the meaning of this phrase as clearly as possible.

In the Time of the Judges

Modern readers of this book will wish to know something about "the people of Israel" as they were in the period before the Monarchy. A term frequently used in the early period is "the tribes of Israel" (Judg. 18:1; 20:2, 10; 21:15; cf. Josh. 24:1). According to George E. Mendenhall ("Tribe," 920), the primary function of these tribes was "the organization of a large and strongly bonded . . . society that could ward off the constant attempts of urban rulers to regain economic and political control of villages." A tribal assembly was held every seven years (Deut. 31:9-13) to affirm a *common faith* by listening to the Covenant Teaching *(Torah)* as in Josh. 8:30-35. At this assembly they would also renew their covenant with Yahweh in a ceremony like that described in Josh. 24:1-28. Their bond of unity was their faith.

From time to time certain of the tribes would join in *common action* against an adversary. Military action would be by the tribal militia called "the men of Israel" (Judg. 7:23; 8:22; 20:11). In one case we hear of six tribes acting in common (5:14-18). In others there were four (6:35) or two (3:15, 27) who campaigned together. Eleven of the tribes act together towards the end of the

11

book in order to punish one of their own tribes for covenant violation. It is at Mizpah in Benjamin that "the chiefs of all the people, of all the tribes of Israel" along with "all the people of Israel" assemble to deal with the crisis caused by the crime at Gibeah (20:1-2).

New Members from Canaan

According to the traditional view, the people of Israel were those who had escaped from Egypt, made their way through the wilderness, and settled in the land of Canaan after having destroyed Canaanite power. This view is now seen to have been greatly oversimplified and even distorted. The more probable picture is that the escapees from Egypt formed a core of the "tribes of Israel" as they entered Canaan. To this core group were added oppressed Canaanites who were alienated from the city-state system. There were debt slaves, sharecroppers, landless farmers, artisans, even rural brigands. These Canaanites threw in their lot with the "tribes of Israel." When, in the covenant ceremony, they took the oath to "serve the LORD" (Josh. 24:18, 21, 24), they were accepted as "descendants" of the tribal ancestors such as Asher, Zebulun, Ephraim, Manasseh, Judah, and so forth, and became part of "the people of Israel (see below, p. 17, "Perspectives," no. 1).

In the Seventh Century B.C.E

When Josiah became king of Judah in 640, "the people of Israel" were widely scattered from Egypt to Mesopotamia as a result of several deportations by Assyria: in 732 (2 Kgs. 15:29), in 721 (2 Kgs. 17:6), and possibly also in 701 for those in "the fortified cities of Judah" outside Jerusalem (2 Kgs. 18:13). In the annals of Sennacherib, the Assyrian king claims with apparent exaggeration to have taken 200,150 prisoners to Nineveh, including the Judean king's daughters, concubines, and court musicians (D. Winton Thomas, ed., *Documents from Old Testament Times* [New York: Harper & Row, 1961], 67).

Judah alone was left in place. The kingdom of Judah itself was confined to the area between Jerusalem on the north and Kadesh-barnea on the south (John Bright, *A History of Israel,* 3rd ed. [Philadelphia: Westminster and London: SCM, 1981], map VII). Josiah's plans to restore the territorial unity of David's kingdom and the unity of the people of Israel were put to an end by his death at the battle of Megiddo in 609 (2 Kgs. 23:29).

"The people of Israel" in the 7th cent. would have meant only the tiny kingdom of Judah and those of the northern kingdom who had been taken into exile. Readers in the 7th cent. would be reminded of *the once and future unity* of the now scattered people (see below, p. 18, "Perspectives," no. 2).

". . . INQUIRED OF THE LORD" (1:1)

The book of Judges begins with a dramatic scene. The whole people is gathered at an unnamed holy place, which may have been Gilgal (cf. Judg. 2:1). They are waiting attentively while a Levitical priest, possibly Phinehas son of Eleazar (cf. 20:28), performs a ceremony to ask for guidance from the LORD (as in Num. 27:21; cf. Judg. 18:5; 1 Sam. 22:10). The time is after the death of both Joshua (Judg. 1:1) and Eleazar the priest (Josh. 24:33). We may assume the presence of "the elders who outlived Joshua and had known all the work which the LORD did for Israel" (Josh. 24:31; cf. Judg. 2:7). The unfinished task that lay before them has been outlined by Joshua: there was "yet very much land to be possessed" (Josh. 13:1), and on that land lived "those nations that remain" (Josh. 23:4). The question was which of the tribes should begin the work of deposing Canaanite power (Judg. 1:1). The answer was that Judah should go first (v. 2).

By artful design, the book of Judges ends with a similar gathering at which all Israel again inquired of the LORD, and then too it was Judah who should go first (20:18; cf. vv. 23, 27). Then, however, the problem was not the threat of Canaanite *power* but rather Canaanite *influence.* A canaanized group in Benjamin had brought the tribes to a bloody civil war. Between the first inquiry and the last is the descending cycle of unfaith in the Promised Land. An appropriate comment on this framework comes from the time of the Exile: "O that you had hearkened to my commandments! Then your peace would have been like a river . . ." (Isa. 48:18; see below, pp. 18-20, "Perspectives," no. 3).

"AGAINST THE CANAANITES" (1:1)

Three Patterns

The "Canaanites" dominate the first chapter of Judges. The term appears more often in this chapter (fourteen times) than in any other chapter of the Hebrew Scriptures. We meet them in three situations:

1. They are *enemies to be opposed and driven from power,* as in the case of the Canaanites in the south who were defeated by Judah (Judg. 1:1-17; the "Canaanites" appear seven times). Here the new society completely displaces the old corrupt one.

2. They are *a minority living among the Israelites,* as in the case of the Canaanites in the territories of Manasseh, Ephraim, and Zebulun, where the Canaanites "persisted in dwelling in that land" (vv. 27, 29, 30). Members of the old society coexist with, but are under the control of, the new society.

3. They are *the dominant group among whom live the Israelites as a minority,* as in the case of the Canaanite society in the north, where Asher and Naphtali lived "among the Canaanites" (vv. 32-33). The new society exists as a leaven which could change the old from within (see below, p. 20, "Perspectives," no. 4).

Canaanite Influence

Outside the first chapter, the term "Canaanites" appears only twice in the rest of the book of Judges (3:3, 5). Indeed, the term appears only six more times in the books following Judges. On the other hand, Canaanite *influence* persists throughout the book of Judges in the form of Canaanite gods, "the Baals and the Ashtaroth" (2:13). This suggests that the term "Canaanites" in Judg. 1 is a kind of code word referring to those forces, structures, and individuals who were seen to be in opposition to the good order of Yahweh. The real adversary was not a whole people, but a way of organizing society.

The Canaanite Way of Organizing Society

In Canaanite society two percent of the population controlled most of the land. Economic administration was for the benefit of the rich at the expense of the poor. Power was in the hands of the royal and urban elite. Urban society existed by sucking wealth from villages and farms. Religious practices included cultic prostitution and child sacrifice, which were supposed to manipulate the gods of fertility for human benefit. Witchcraft was practiced in order to make use of the supposed power of the spirits of the dead. Incestual family relations may have been related to the fertility cult. All of these practices and the social structures behind them were related to "serving the Baals and the Ashtaroth." In the words of a sociological study of ancient Israel,

> When Israel used the cipher "Canaan-Canaanite(s)" to des- ignate those enemies, precise socioeconomic and political groupings and functionaries within the hierarchic system were meant: "Canaanite kings," "Canaanite armies," "Canaanite merchants," "Canaanite landowners and over- seers," "Canaanite city-state officials," and "Canaanite gods and cults and their priestly functionaries." . . . It was the political-cultic complex as a totality that was abhorred and opposed. (Norman K. Gottwald, *The Tribes of Yahweh*, 586-87)

A Way of Death

With this background we can better understand the stern words of Covenant Teaching given to the Israelites who lived in the land of Canaan:

> . . . you shall not do as they do in the land of Canaan. . . . You shall not walk in their statutes. You shall do my ordi- nances . . . and walk in them . . . by doing which a man shall live. (Lev. 18:3-5)

The political, ethical, and spiritual way which Israel learned from Yahweh through Moses was a prescription for life intended for the individual, the family, and the nation. The "Canaanite" way was a formula for death. It was, as the Thai expression goes, "a burden on the land" *(nak paendin)*. Other descriptions of the effects of this way of life are that it "polluted" the land, making it unfit for human habitation (Jer. 3:2; cf. Hos. 4:3), or that it caused such nausea that the land "vomited out its inhabitants" like poisoned food (Lev. 18:24-25).

The Way of Death in Israel

The book of Judges chronicles the repeated political, ethical, and spiritual capitulation of the Israelites to the "Canaanite" way of death. Again and again they "did what was evil in the sight of the LORD, forgetting the LORD their God, and serving the Baals and the Asheroth" (Judg. 3:7). As the book comes to a close in a scene like that at the beginning (cf. 1:1; 20:18), the adversary is not the Canaanites but a canaanized group in Benjamin (see below, pp. 20-21, "Perspectives," no. 5).

1. A Note on Translation: Inhabitants, or Rulers?

The Hebrew verb *yashab,* which occurs frequently in Judg. 1, may be translated in the context of this chapter in two ways: (a) to dwell in a place, and (b) to rule over a place, that is, to sit in a position of authority over it. The verb occurs here in two forms: the finite verb and the participle. After a careful study of the uses of this verb, Norman K. Gottwald has concluded that the participial form should be translated as "rulers" instead of the usual translation "inhabitants" (Judg. 1:19), or the ones "who inhabited" (v. 17) or "who dwelt" in a certain place (v. 21). The finite verb form should be translated as "dwell." An example of the two meanings in a single verse is found in 1:21: "But the people of Benjamin did not drive out the Jebusites *who dwelt in*" Jerusalem [i.e., the Jebusite *rulers*]; so the Jebusites have *dwelt* with the people of Benjamin in Jerusalem to this day."

Following this interpretation, we find references to the "rulers" of Hebron (Judg. 1:10), Debir (v. 11), Zephath (v. 17), the plain (v. 19), Jerusalem (v. 21), Beth-shean, Taanach, Ibleam, Megiddo (v. 27), Gezer (v. 29), Kitron, Nahalol (v. 30), Acco, Sidon, Ahlab, Achzib, Helbah, Aphik, Rehob (v. 31), Beth-shemesh, Beth-anath (v. 33). According to Gottwald (*The Tribes of Yahweh,* 531-33), the term *yashab* in the participial form in this context means "ruling oppressively" with harsh injustice. These rulers were, he says, "leaders in the imperial-feudal statist system of social organization, with primary reference to enemy kings," but including princes, military commanders, and those in authority.

2. *Note on Translation: "Drive out," or "Drive out of Power"?*

The causative form of another verb, *yarash* (hiphil), also occurs frequently in this chapter (see E. John Hamlin, *Inheriting the Land*, 9-10, for a discussion of this verb). The RSV translates the verb as "drive out" in Judg. 1:19, 21, 27-33. This translation is acceptable if we specify the meaning "to drive out from power" and understand the object of the verb to be the rulers described above. To quote from Gottwald,

> The issue . . . is *not so much who lives in the cities and regions as who exercises control*. . . . It is not a matter of driving out all inhabitants but of expelling kings and rulers, of abolishing royal-aristocratic-feudal control. . . . Where Israel could not drive out the rulers and their administrative apparatus extending into the countryside . . . it became difficult for the Israelite communities to take root or to persist. (*The Tribes of Yahweh*, 528)

PERSPECTIVES

1. *The People of God (see above, pp. 11-12)*

The Israelites in the period before the Monarchy were not just any people. They were the "people of the LORD" (Judg. 5:11; cf. 11:23). This special relationship with "the God of Israel" (5:3; 6:8) gives the dramatic narratives of the book of Judges their distinctive character. "The people of Israel" were, it was believed, chosen to fulfil a divine purpose in the land of Canaan (Deut. 4:5-8), and indeed in the whole earth (Gen. 12:3; Exod. 19:5-6; see below, pp. 60-61, on Israel's "mission identity"). Thus the dramatic narrative focuses "less upon the political realities than upon the hidden theological purposes which are seen to have been at work" (Ronald E. Clements, *Old Testament Theology*, 84). The risks of life in the Promised Land are aspects of the constant interaction between Yahweh, "the LORD of all the earth" (Josh. 3:11), and his faithful yet faithless people.

2. One People (see above, pp. 12-13)

A united "people of Israel" at the beginning of the book of Judges calls to mind the "one flock, one shepherd" (John 10:16; cf. 17:21) which is God's will and purpose for his people in the world, as well as the modern ecumenical movement.

3. Inquiring of the Lord (see above, p. 13)

A parallel to all Israel's inquiring of the LORD, at the beginning and end of the book of Judges, may be seen in David's similar inquiry at the beginning of the Monarchy (1 Sam. 22:9-10, 15) and Josiah's at the height of his reform movement (2 Kgs. 22:13). Following the pattern of the book of Judges, these two acts of inquiry enclose Israel's history of faith and unfaith in the period of the Monarchy.

Learning God's will is a mysterious process beset with problems. As recorded in the Hebrew Scriptures, the priests and prophets mediated God's answers to those who sought God's guidance. In early practice, the *priests* were to "inquire . . . by the judgment of the Urim before the LORD" (Num. 27:21). In later times this method, which depended on manipulation of these objects (something like throwing dice), was considered too crude and not specific enough. The priests themselves were responsible for interpreting the Covenant Teaching (Jer. 2:8; RSV "law"). The priest was seen as a "messenger of the LORD of hosts" (Mal. 2:7), with "true instruction . . . in his mouth" (v. 6). The *prophets* had a more direct access to God through dreams or visions (1 Kgs. 22:17-22; Amos 9:1; Isa. 6:1; Jer. 23:18).

One problem was *corrupt mediators*. Priests could and did become corrupt, give false interpretations of God's will (Hos. 4:6), and "teach for hire" (Mic. 3:11). "False" prophets were known to "divine for money" (Mic. 3:11). Even though they prophesied in God's name and claimed to have had dreams and visions (Jer. 23:25-27), they gave the people "vain hopes" of victory and prosperity (vv. 16-17). The answer given Ahaz of Israel by the four hundred prophets was the opposite of that given by Micaiah (1 Kgs. 22:6, 17).

A second problem was that Israel's kings *inquired of the wrong god.* Ahaziah of Israel sent messengers to "inquire of Baal-zebub, the god of Ekron," as though there were "no god in Israel to inquire of his word" (2 Kgs. 1:16). Shallum, Menahem, or Pekah of Israel may have been in Hosea's mind when he said in Yahweh's name: "My people inquire of a thing of wood, and their staff gives them oracles" (Hos. 4:12). These kings made alliances with Egypt against Assyria, or with Assyria against Egypt (Hos. 7:11), and ambitious citizens made plots to assassinate kings, not by calling on Yahweh (7:7) or by seeking his will (8:4). Isaiah saw leaders and people of Judah consulting "the dead on behalf of the living" in a time of "distress and darkness, the gloom of anguish" (Isa. 8:19, 22). He condemned Hezekiah for joining an anti-Assyrian alliance at what seemed like the right time to regain independence for all Israel, both north and south, "without asking" for Yahweh's counsel (Isa. 30:1-3; cf. 31:1-3).

In the days of Jehoiakim, the Scribe would have seen princes, prophets, and inhabitants of Jerusalem seeking the guidance of "the sun and the moon and all the host of heaven" instead of Yahweh (Jer. 8:1-2). The consequence was theft, murder, adultery, false oaths, worship of other gods (Jer. 7:9), "shedding innocent blood, . . . oppression and violence" (22:17), as well as persecution of true prophets who dared to speak words of judgment (26:20-23).

Invitation to the Powerless. It was during the exile in Babylon, after the nation had been broken by "the heat of his anger and the might of battle . . . [and] fire round about" (Isa. 42:25), that a word came to the remnant of survivors from the prophet of the Exile (Isa. 45:20). He appealed to them to "seek the LORD while he may be found" (Isa. 55:6) and to submit their collective wills to the One whose thoughts and ways are "higher" than those of individuals or nations (vv. 8-9).

Inquiring of the Lord Today. The issue is very relevant for today. Although we do not use mechanical devices like a throw of dice for making important decisions, we do have interpreters of God's word ("priests") and those who attempt to apply this word to particular situations ("prophets"). Problems of false mediators and false gods are still with us. "Inquiring of the LORD" is still corrupted by the self-interest of individuals and corporate structures.

The tension between seeking the LORD in faith, on the one

19

hand, and making specific decisions about alliances, choosing leaders, and ordering our personal and corporate lives, on the other hand, is still with us. It is always the right time to "seek the LORD while he may be found" (Isa. 55:6).

4. *Three Models for Christians in Society (see above, p. 14)*

In the varied situations in which Israel related to the Canaanites, we may discern three models for the existence of Christians in today's societies and cultures.

a. *A "Christian" state* may be established according to covenantal principles, like that established in Josh. 24. In this kind of state there would be perfect obedience to the LORD of the Covenant, perfect security for the people of God, and no room for dissent or divergence.

b. *A pluralistic society with a dominant Christian tradition* is the second model. In biblical history we see that, with changing circumstances, the "Canaanites" became an important reality in a society originally established on covenantal principles. This began in the time of David, became more risky in the time of Solomon, and took the form of a deep sickness in both the northern and southern kingdoms. Canaanite influence corrupted leaders and the people so that they forgot their founding covenantal principles.

c. The third model is *a Christian minority in a society organized on noncovenantal principles.* In the Bible we find this in the exilic period, when the faithful remnant lived as aliens in the midst of an oppressive society. This model reappears when Christians are a small minority in a different dominant culture, like the situations of Christians in Pakistan or Thailand. The title of a book by William Stringfellow suggests that this may also be true in what might at one time have been considered a "Christian land": *An Ethic for Christians and Other Aliens in a Strange Land.*

5. *The Battle against Evil (see above, pp. 15-16)*

The Hebrew *laham,* translated as "fight against," is used five times in the first nine verses of Judges to describe the victorious struggle of the tribe of Judah against the Canaanite way of death (Judg. 1:1, 3, 5, 8, 9). The same word describes the attacks of oppressors on Israel (11:4; "make war") and Yahweh's intervention on behalf of Israel (Josh. 10:14, 42).

The preeminence of Judah appears prominently in the book of Revelation. As in the book of Judges the tribe of Judah is designated as the leader in the warfare against "the Canaanites," so in Revelation the "Lion of the tribe of Judah" is the only one worthy to open the scroll with its seven seals which are to bring judgment on the forces of evil and death in the world (Rev. 5:5).

However, the author of Revelation gives the narrative a surprising turn. The Lion in turn becomes "the Lamb who was slain" (Rev. 5:12). By his death did this Lion/Lamb ransom people "for God from every tribe and tongue and people and nation" to be "a kingdom and priests to our God" (Rev. 5:9-10). In this vision from the time of the Roman persecution, the weapon that would bring victory over the power of evil and win over many to the covenant way of life was suffering love.

There are many ways of carrying on the struggle against evil. Each must involve strategy and tactics which depend on the situation. One group of concerned people decided that "the trend . . . toward a permanent urban underclass is unacceptable" and that "breaking the cycle of poverty that afflicts *some* of us should be a goal of surpassing importance to *all* of us." Their strategy to oppose what we might term this "Canaanite way of death" is to purchase, clean, and renovate deteriorated buildings in urban areas for low income residents ("Year of the Jubilee," letter from Jubilee Housing, Inc., Washington, D.C., 1983, 3, 5).

FAITHFUL JUDAH
Judges 1:2-21

JUDAH FIRST

The Scribe shows his preference for Judah by positioning that tribe at the beginning of the prologue. This is not surprising in view of the historical context in which he wrote. Judah was the sole surviving tribe still on the land. This preference is the more remarkable in view of the deep corruption of Judah and Jerusalem at the time. He devotes twenty verses to Judah (Judg. 1:2-21), as compared with thirteen for the northern tribes (vv. 22-34). Furthermore his description shows Judah as a faithful follower of Joshua and Moses in contrast to the others.

This preference for Judah in the prologue and epilogue reveals a marked difference between the books of Judges and Joshua. In the latter the Ephraimite Joshua, servant of Moses, is the sole and undisputed leader in military, civic, and religious affairs. In Judges the southern tribe of Judah is designated to take the initiative in the unfinished task of establishing the reign of God in the land and, at the end, of punishing the guilty within Israel (see below, p. 35, "Perspectives," no. 1).

A LOOK AT THE STRUCTURE

The Judah narrative is structured around *three general summary statements* in which Judah's claim to the territory allotted to it is confirmed. *Five military victories* north to south describe the cleansing of the land from Canaanite influence. Among these summaries and victories is a series of *seven anecdotal remarks* giving clues as to the intention of the author.

22

Summaries

1. The LORD grants the entire territory to Judah (v. 2).
2. Judah fights against the rulers of the hill country, Negeb, and lowlands (v. 9).
3. With the LORD's help Judah takes control of the hill country, but is not able to wrest power from the rulers of the coastal areas because of their superior armaments (v. 19).

Victories

1. Over the Canaanites and Perizzites at Bezek (vv. 4-5).
2. Over the rulers of Jerusalem (v. 8).
3. Over the three Canaanite rulers of Hebron (v. 10).
4. Over the rulers of Debir (vv. 11-13).
5. Over the rulers of Zephath/Hormah (v. 17).

Anecdotal Remarks

1. Judah invites Simeon to join in the campaign (v. 3).
2. Adoni-bezek is captured, punished, and dies in Jerusalem (vv. 6-7).
3. Achsah asks for and receives the springs at Debir as a gift from her father (vv. 14-15).
4. The Kenites settle in the Negeb near Arad (v. 16).
5. Judah captures the three cities of the coastal plain (v. 18).
6. Hebron is given to Caleb (v. 20).
7. Unlike Judah, the Benjaminites do not drive the Jebusite rulers of Jerusalem from power, but live among them (v. 21).

Victory over the Canaanites and Perizzites (1:4-5)

Judah's first encounter is with these two peoples, which the Scribe emphasizes by mentioning them twice. Their significance will be understood only in the light of a wider context. The only other references to these two peoples together in the Old Testament suggest that Yahweh's direct intervention to give Judah victory (v. 4) was not to force them out of the land in order to make room for Judah and the other tribes of Israel, but to make possible a new

23

society from which blessing might spread to "all the families of the earth" (Gen. 12:3).

When Abraham and Lot were having difficulties over grazing land for their cattle, "the Canaanites and the Perizzites dwelt in the land" (Gen. 13:7), presumably in the region of Bethel. There is no hint of tension or conflict between Abraham and these folk. Abraham is called to "live among them, to practice and believe the promise . . . to permit the reality of blessing to be at work" (Walter Brueggemann, *Genesis*. Interpretation [Atlanta: John Knox, 1982], 124).

The situation is radically different in Gen. 34. This time the Canaanites and Perizzites are rulers of the area around Shechem (Gen. 34:30; see translation note above, p. 16, for "rulers" instead of "inhabitants"). They are in a position to destroy Jacob and his household (i.e., Israel). The causes of this tension and potential conflict are rape (Gen. 34:2), love across cultural lines (v. 3), greed (v. 23), trickery, and bad faith (vv. 25-27), which involved both Israel, on the one side, and the Canaanites and Perizzites, on the other. No "blessing" is possible under these conditions.

The material in Genesis is arranged in such a way as to suggest that Israel itself needed cleansing in this affair. Following the incident at Shechem, we find Jacob and his family putting away the "foreign [i.e., Canaanite] gods" that were "among" them, as well as their golden jewelry (Gen. 35:2, 4). They move away from the territory ruled by the Canaanites and Perizzites to Bethel (Gen. 35:1, 3), where they receive a new identity (v. 10) and hear again God's promise to give them the land (v. 12; cf. Gen. 12:2), from which the flow of the energy of blessing for the nations could begin again.

The Scribe's account of victory over "the Canaanites and the Perizzites" suggests a similar divinely appointed opportunity for Judah to put away Canaanite gods and the Canaanite "way of death" (see above, pp. 15-16) which frustrate God's purpose of blessing for the nations.

ADONI-BEZEK—THE LAST CANAANITE KING
IN THE SOUTH (1:4-7)

Adoni-bezek was the king of the Canaanites and Perizzites, captured by Judah after the battle of Bezek. His captors either took him, or allowed his people to take him, to Jerusalem where he died. The meaning of this brief anecdote in the midst of the Judah story is obscure to the casual reader. If we begin by assuming, with the principles of canonical criticism, that the book of Judges should be taken as a whole, we should look for some relationship with the idea of kingship which appears in the closing chapters: "In those days there was no king in Israel; every man did what was right in his own eyes" (Judg. 21:25).

A Title?

"Adoni" may have been a title instead of a name. It is a Hebrew word which means "my lord." It was used in addressing a person of rank or position, as "my lord Moses" (*adoni Moshe,* Num. 11:28), "my lord Joab" (2 Sam. 11:11), "my lord Elijah" (1 Kgs. 18:7), or "my lord the king" (1 Sam. 24:8). With a slight change of the final vowel, the word may designate a high official, as Joseph, "the lord of the land" (*adoney ha'arets,* Gen. 42:30), or a landowner like "Shemer, the owner of the hill" (*adoney hahar,* 1 Kgs. 16:24).

Prince of Bezek?

If Bezek is the name of a place, as seems likely from Judg. 1:4, "Adoni-bezek" would designate a ruler or high official in a place called Bezek, something like the Prince of Wales, or the Duke of Gloucester, or the Prince of Chiang Mai in Thailand. The problem is that the only two possible locations thus far suggested do not fit the geographical situation in Judg. 1:1-21.

The only other Bezek in the Hebrew Scriptures is the modern Khirbet Ibziq, the town 20 km. (12 mi.) north of Shechem where Saul gathered his forces before crossing the Jordan River to attack the Ammonites (1 Sam. 11:8). Some scholars believe that this was the Bezek in Judg. 1:4, and that Judah crossed the Jordan at this northern point before going south to Hebron (Yohanan Aharoni and Michael Avi-Yonah, *The Macmillan Bible Atlas,* 45, map 57). Those who accept this must explain why Adoni-bezek was taken by his allies to Jerusalem from such a northern place. There is no indication that the rulers of Jerusalem ever held sway over the area north of Shechem.

The other location proposed by some scholars because of the similar spelling is the modern Khirbet Bezqa, near Gezer in the lowlands near the coastal plain (Robert G. Boling, *Judges,* 55). Two problems make this location doubtful: (1) it lies in the territory assigned to Ephraim instead of Judah (cf. Judg. 1:3), and (2) it is too far from and unrelated to Jerusalem. In conclusion, it seems best to leave the location of this Bezek as an unknown and perhaps unimportant part of the narrative in Judg. 1.

A Taunt Name?

If Bezek is primarily the name of an individual rather than a place, "Adoni-bezek" would mean "my lord Bezek" or "the honorable Bezek." We cannot rule out the possibility that Bezek is a satirical name invented or altered from an original. An Aramaic cognate means "pebble" (J. Alberto Soggin, *Judges,* 21; George F. Moore, *Judges,* 15), so "my lord Pebble" might have been a derisive nickname.

If we divide the Hebrew word *bezeq* into two parts, the Hebrew letter *b* is a preposition which may be translated "in" or "with." The other part of the term is a word *zeq,* which means "chain" or "fetter." The combination of the preposition with the noun in the plural *(bazziqqim)* means "in chains" (Isa. 45:14; Nah. 3:10) or "with chains" (Ps. 149:8). This interpretation of the name Adoni-bezek would have a double sense: "my lord *with* a chain," that is, the one who bound the seventy kings, or "my lord *in* a chain," the one bound in chains by Judah.

The Last Canaanite King in Jerusalem

Another way to look at the significance of Adoni-bezek is in relationship to the city of Jerusalem, where he was taken after his humiliating treatment and where he died. Only two Canaanite kings of this city are mentioned by name in the Hebrew Scriptures. The first is Melchizedek, "king of Salem . . . priest of God Most High" (Gen. 14:18 [Salem is traditionally identified with Jerusalem; cf. Ps. 76:2]), who blessed Abraham. The other is Adoni-zedek, king of Jerusalem and leader of a coalition of southern kings who tried to put an end to Joshua's campaign in

26

Canaan (Josh. 10:3; 12:10). Whether or not we see Adoni-bezek as the princely son of Adoni-zedek (Judah J. Slotki, "Judges," 157), we are justified in seeing some connection between these two Jerusalem rulers and Adoni-bezek, a third king of Jerusalem.

A Desacralized Priest-King

Now let us look at Adoni-bezek's remark that he cut off the thumbs and great toes of seventy kings but that God had "requited" him by having his own thumbs and great toes cut off (Judg. 1:7). This kind of mutilation is not unknown in the ancient world. Records tell us that the Athenians cut off the thumbs of their prisoners of war, and that Hannibal of Carthage cut off the great toes of his captives (John Gray, *Joshua, Judges, Ruth,* 236).

At the consecration ceremony for the temple priests in Jerusalem, the thumbs and great toes of priests were daubed with sacrificial blood (Exod. 29:20; Lev. 8:23). In all likelihood the thumb represented the hands, which would perform sacrifices (Lev. 7:30; 8:14, 26-27) and invoke divine blessing on the people (Lev. 9:22). The great toe likewise represented the feet of the one who would stand in the holy place (Num. 16:9; 1 Chron. 23:30; Ps. 24:3). We know from royal legends of the Canaanites discovered at Ras Shamra that Canaanite kings were also priests, like Melchizedek (Gen. 14:18; Gray, 236). Their holy tasks included offering sacrifices, blessing the people, and standing in the holy places. Thus the thumbs and great toes of the Canaanite kings in Judg. 1:7 would have sacral significance.

When Adoni-bezek cut off the thumbs and great toes of the "seventy" (code word for "all") kings of southern Canaan, he made it impossible for them to be "sacred kings" any more. And when the tribe of Judah cut off Adoni-bezek's own thumbs and great toes, that was the end of the Canaanite order of sacred kings. What had begun as a blessing (Gen. 14:18-19) had become an obstacle to God's good order. A corrupted Canaanite social order with false claims to divine sanction came to an end with the dethroning of this last Canaanite king in the south (see below, p. 81, for kings in the north; see also below, pp. 35-36, "Perspectives," no. 2).

We can get some idea of the Scribe's view of the kingship in Israel from subsequent chapters of Judges. Gideon refused the offer of kingship on the grounds that Yahweh was king (Judg. 8:22-23). What Gideon refused, his son Abimelech seized by killing his seventy brothers, as Adoni-bezek had mutilated his seventy rivals (9:5-6). As God had "requited" (1:7) the last Canaanite king in southern Canaan, so was the crime of the "canaanized" Abimelech "requited" (9:56). Jotham's parable (Judg. 9:8-20) should be seen as an attack on the *canaanized* kingship.

THE CLEANSING OF JERUSALEM AND HEBRON

Key Victories

The victories at Jerusalem and Hebron at the beginning of this section (1:8, 10), balanced by the two anecdotal remarks in reverse order about Hebron and Jerusalem at the end (vv. 20-21), suggest an artful framework for the entire Judah narrative.

A Temporary Cleansing: Jerusalem (1:8)

The supporting structure of the Canaanite social order was destroyed when the Judahites "fought against" Jerusalem, "took" it, killed its inhabitants, and "set the city on fire." The verbs used by the Scribe suggest a relationship between his brief reference to a victory over Jerusalem and Joshua's victories over the cities of Judah (Josh. 10:28-39). Jerusalem was the one city not subdued in Joshua's southern campaign. The note in Judg. 1:8 may refer to an indecisive victory which did not result in a change of the power structure. Jerusalem probably remained as an enclave in a heavily settled Israelite area right up to David's successful attack (2 Sam. 5:6-8). There may have been "a formal or a de facto recognition of the dominance of . . . the intertribal Israelite confederation" (Norman K. Gottwald, *The Tribes of Yahweh,* 570).

Following Judg. 1:21 Jerusalem is absent from the Judges narratives until the last chapters. The meaning of the reference to the Benjaminites in 1:21 becomes clear when we look at Jerusalem as it appears in 19:10-12. The Levite refuses to spend the night in Jebus (that is, Jerusalem), "the city of foreigners, who do not belong to the people of Israel" (Judg. 19:12). He goes on to pass the night in Gibeah where the Benjaminites commit the terrible crime which plunges Israel into civil war (19:16, 22-26). It was the continued association of Benjaminites (1:21) with the "foreigners" in Jerusalem and their "foreign gods" (cf. Judg. 10:16; Deut. 31:16) that alienated them from their fellow Israelites (Judg. 19:30; 20:6; 21:1; see below, pp. 36-37, "Perspectives," no. 3).

Note on Fire in the Promised Land

The particular Hebrew idiom which is translated as "set on fire" (Judg. 1:8) is used again in the book of Judges only of the action of the tribes of Israel against the towns of Benjamin (20:48). Both cases involve a cleansing action against Canaanite corruptions, first Canaanite Jerusalem and then a canaanized Benjamin. The only other city to be burned with fire in Judges is Laish (18:27). This is portrayed as a savage act of aggression against a peaceful people.

Another kind of fire, not of cleansing but of revenge and struggle for power, is found in the story of Abimelech, the canaanized king. Jotham's curse was that fire would flare out of Abimelech's cruel anger to devour the citizens of Shechem, and that fire would flare out of their desire for revenge to consume Abimelech (9:20).

Note on the Edge of the Sword in the Promised Land

The Scribe uses the idiom to "smite with the edge of the sword" only of Jerusalem (Judg. 1:8) and Bethel (1:25) in the prologue, and Laish/Dan (18:27), Gibeah of Benjamin (20:37), and Jabesh-gilead (21:10) in the epilogue. Bethel and Dan later became shrine cities designed to rival and even supplant Jerusalem (1 Kgs. 12:29; cf. 2 Kgs. 10:29). They became centers of canaanization (Amos 5:5; 8:14). Both the Gibeah and the Jabesh-gilead incidents were cruel acts of civil war. Nothing is said in these five references about Yahweh's intervention or command. The outcome seems to say that the violence was without any lasting cleansing effect.

The End of Tyranny at Hebron (1:10)

Hebron, where Abraham had met God in visions (Gen. 13:18; 15:1; 18:1), and where he had buried Sarah (Gen. 23:2, 19) among Hittite friends (23:6), had become the city of King Hoham, the enemy of Joshua (Josh. 10:3), and later of the three tyrants, Sheshai, Ahiman, and Talmai. The Scribe does not describe them as "descendants of Anak" as in previous accounts (Num. 13:22; Josh. 15:14), but as "Canaanites" (Judg. 1:10). He thus relates them to the "Canaanite way of death" (see above, pp. 15-16).

The Anakim were a pre-Israelite tribe in Palestine whose leaders bore Semitic names. Their presence around 2000 B.C.E. is attested by Egyptian curse texts bearing the names of the pharaoh's enemies (R. F. Schnell, "Anak," *IDB* 1:123). In Hebrew thought the Anakim were descended from the Nephilim (Num. 13:33), who were legendary half-human, half-divine beings (Gen. 6:4). They were of gigantic height (Deut. 2:10, 21) and strength, so that they became symbols of irresistible power. "Who can stand before the sons of Anak?" was the common saying (Deut. 9:2; see below, p. 37, "Perspectives," no. 4).

Hebron may well be a hidden pointer to David. It reappears only once in the book of Judges after the prologue when the Danite Samson deposits the gates of the Philistine city of Gaza on "the top of the hill that is before Hebron" (Judg. 16:3); this is probably the site of David's coronation (2 Sam. 5:3) and palace. Perhaps we may see in this account of Samson's exploit a kind of "prophetic" action, with an allusion for the 7th cent. reader to David's future victories over the Philistines (2 Sam. 5:25; 8:1). Hebron had to be cleansed of tyranny and injustice before David could rise to power there.

Note on the Original Name of Hebron

The original name of Hebron was Kiriath-arba, the "City of Arba" (Josh. 15:13), named for its legendary founder (Josh. 14:15), the "greatest man" (Heb. *adam gadol*) of the tribe and ancestor of the Anakim (Josh. 15:13). It is possible that *arba*, which means "four," was originally the name of a god of the four phases of the moon (Charles F. Burney, *The Book of Judges*, 43-44).

HARMONY AT DEBIR (1:11-15)

Debir, City of Right Relationships

The Scribe has made artful use of the Debir narrative from Josh. 15:15-19 to introduce the theme of original right relationships in the tribe of Judah (see E. John Hamlin, *Inheriting the Land,* 123-24, for the different function of the Debir narrative in Joshua). This theme passage stands in sharp contrast to the many broken relationships described in subsequent narratives (see Edith T. A. Davidson, "Intricacy, Design, and Cunning in the Book of Judges," 19-24).

Brotherly Harmony

Caleb generously allowed his junior officer ("younger brother," Judg. 1:13; Boling, *Judges,* 56) to have the honor of taking and presumably governing Debir. We may contrast this harmonious fraternal relationship in Judah with Ephraim's bitter complaints against Gideon of Manasseh (8:1) and Jephthah the Gileadite (12:1). Civil war was the result (12:4-6). Abimelech slaughtered seventy brothers (9:5), was cursed by Jotham, his younger brother (9:20, 57), and was betrayed by Gaal, a fellow Shechemite (9:26-29). The bloody war between Benjamin and the other tribes with which the book of Judges closes (ch. 20) shows the final deterioration among the northern tribes of the brotherly harmony which was visible at Debir.

Harmony between Father and Daughter

Unlike the other Israelites, who gave their daughters in marriage to Canaanite men (3:6), Caleb was a good father who arranged for his daughter's marriage with a man of Judah. Caleb's provision for Achsah's marriage to Othniel represents an ideal beginning. Subsequent examples tell how other father-daughter relationships went from bad to worse.

Jephthah killed his daughter in fulfillment of a rash vow (11:39), as fathers were doing in the reign of Jehoiakim (Jer. 7:31). The Philistine father of Samson's first wife gave her to

31

Samson's best man (Judg. 15:1-2). The prophets had said that would happen in Israel (2 Sam. 12:11; Amos 7:17; Jer. 8:10; cf. Deut. 28:30). The father of the Levite's concubine kept her husband drinking and feasting for five days quite unconcerned for his daughter's well-being (Judg. 19:4-9), just as the unthinking rich had done in the days of Isaiah (Isa. 5:11-12, 22; 28:1, 7-8), with no thought for "the ruin of Joseph" (Amos 6:6) nor any tears for "the virgin daughter of my people" (Jer. 14:17). The men of Israel vowed not to give their daughters in marriage to any from the tribe of Benjamin because of the crime committed in Gibeah (Judg. 21:1; cf. Jer. 7:34).

Harmony between Wife and Husband

Achsah "came" of her own accord to her husband's side (Judg. 1:14). In her wisdom she made sure that her family would have watered fields for cultivation of crops (cf. Prov. 31:10-31). In the Scribe's arrangement Othniel is the only deliverer of Israel from the tribe of Judah (Judg. 3:9). Following this model wife-husband relationship, the rest of the book of Judges demonstrates a steady degeneration in such relationships.

Samson's Philistine wife became his temptress (14:15-17), while Samson left his bride in a fit of anger at their wedding party (14:19). Delilah betrayed Samson (16:4-21). The Levite callously gave his wife-concubine to the mob of Gibeah and remained in the house until morning while they committed a mass rape and murder (19:25-26).

The beginning and the end of Judges are ironically balanced by the picture of a woman on a donkey. In the prologue Achsah is happily riding on her own donkey to meet her hero husband (1:14). In the epilogue a violated woman's body is draped over another donkey (19:28; Davidson, ix, 20; see below, p. 38, "Perspectives," no. 5).

Blessing on the Land

Caleb showed he was a good father by giving his daughter and son-in-law a blessing-present (the Hebrew word in Judg. 1:15 is *berakah,* which may be translated either as "gift" [Gen. 33:11] or as "blessing" [Gen. 27:35, 41]). Caleb's blessing-present may be compared with Isaac's blessing given to Jacob: "a field which the LORD has blessed . . . the dew of heaven . . . the fatness of the earth, and plenty of grain and wine . . ." (Gen. 27:27-28). The land of Canaan was "a plentiful land," God's gift to Israel "to enjoy its fruits and its good things" (Jer. 2:7; cf. Deut. 8:7; 11:11).

Contrast this idyllic picture with later conditions. We find crops being destroyed by enemies (Judg. 6:3-4), robbery in the country-side (9:25), drunken feasting in the fields leading to plans for revenge (v. 27), fields used for ambush instead of producing "sweetness and good fruit" (v. 43; cf. v. 11), and a city sown with salt (v. 45). We see Samson burning the grain fields of the Philistines (15:5) and the Danites burning Laish with fire, even though the people were "quiet and unsuspecting" (18:27).

THE FINAL CLEANSING (1:17)

"The Canaanites" appear in this verse for the last time in the Judah story (Judg. 1:1-21). The destruction *(herem)* of Zephath at the extreme southern boundary of Judah's territory brings to a climax the symbolic cleansing of the whole territory from the defilement of Canaanite ways (cf. Lev. 18:25, 27; see Hamlin, *Inheriting the Land,* 52-54, 90-92). Of all the post-Joshua generation, Judah alone is represented as having made a complete break with Canaanite "abominable practices" (Deut. 18:9).

The Scribe has artfully contrasted this final cleansing of the land at the beginning with the pollution of the land at the end of Judges. The only time he uses the word *herem* again in the book of Judges is to describe the "utter destruction" of the entire population of the Israelite city of Jabesh-gilead (Judg. 21:11). The Scribe has provided his readers with a mirror in which to see themselves with "the lifeblood of guiltless poor" on their clothing (Jer. 2:34).

Note on Zephath

Zephath is probably to be located at Khirbet Garrah (Tel Ira) on the southern border of Judah. Although Beersheba was the capital of the Negeb of Judah in David's time, the fortified city of Khirbet Garrah was larger and much more impressive than all its neighboring settlements, dominating the whole region (Yohanan Aharoni, *The Land of the Bible,* 216, 353).

Note on Hormah

Hormah was probably at nearby Khirbet Meshash, about 12 km. (8 mi.) east of Beersheba. Before the monarchy it was the largest unfortified tribal settlement of the whole area. Hormah was known by the Egyptians as early as 2000 B.C.E. and appears in the list of Joshua's victories (Josh. 12:14) and David's early campaigns (1 Sam. 30:30). At the beginning of David's reign the Israelite settlement at Khirbet Meshash (Hormah) was transferred to Khirbet Garrah (Zephath). Presumably at this time the name was also changed from Zephath to Hormah. This is the tradition recalled by the Scribe (Judg. 1:17; Aharoni, *The Land of the Bible,* 206, 216).

We do not know the meaning of the pre-Israelite name of Hormah. In Hebrew it is derived from the word *herem,* and could be translated as "destruction" (Num. 21:3 mg). A different meaning is also possible: a place or object dedicated to God. This second meaning is preserved in the Arabic word *harem,* meaning both the place and the persons reserved for the use of the master. The double meaning of Hormah would carry a warning to alert readers during the reign of Jehoiakim: this land must be cleansed of the "pollutions" of the Canaanites, or it will be destroyed!

JUDAH'S ONE FAILURE (1:19)

The territory allotted to Judah (Judg. 1:3) included not only the hill country, the Negeb, and the lowland (v. 9), but also the coastal plain (Josh. 15:45-47). The "regions of the Philistines" were included in the unfinished task left by Joshua (Josh. 13:2-3). The Scribe was probably making use of an old tradition of a temporary victory over three of the five future Philistine cities (Judg. 1:18; the LXX text tells us that Judah did *not* conquer the cities of the plain). Only superior Philistine or "pre-Philistine" armaments (see below, pp. 49, 79-80) prevented Judah from driving "the inhabitants [rulers] of the plain" from their positions of power (Judg. 1:19).

34

It is possible that this tradition originally referred to an attack on the pre-Philistine Canaanites who lived on the plain, and later made incursions into the central highlands "in the days of Shamgar, son of Anath" (3:31; 5:6; cf. 3:1, 3; Boling, *Judges,* 90; see below, pp. 79-80).

The Scribe mentions only three of the five Philistine cities (listed in Josh. 13:3). These may have been the only ones still in existence in his time, as we may gather from the list in Jer. 25:20 (cf. Zech. 9:5-6; and earlier lists of four, Amos 1:6-8; Zeph. 2:4).

More likely the Scribe was pointing his readers forward to the Samson stories in which Timnah in the vicinity of Ekron (Judg. 14:1), Ashkelon (v. 19), and Gaza (16:1) figure prominently. This brief notice about the frustrated victory in the Philistine plain is like a motif in an overture which anticipates a major development of the theme later in the opera. From a theological point of view, the Samson stories are vivid illustrations of the unhappy consequences of Judah's failure to remove the Philistines from power, even though it was not strictly speaking Judah's fault. This is the one blemish on the otherwise perfect record of Judah as given us by the Scribe.

PERSPECTIVES

1. Hope from Judah (see above, p. 22)

The hope of Israel's restoration by a future leader from the tribe of Judah, anticipated by the Scribe in the book of Judges before the fall of Jerusalem (587 B.C.E.), lived on during the exile of the people of Judah in Babylon. The mission of the Servant of the LORD, presumably from Judah, was "to raise up the tribes of Jacob and to restore the preserved of Israel" (Isa. 49:6). New Testament readers will think of the Son of David who "was sent . . . to the lost sheep of the house of Israel" (Matt. 15:24; cf. 10:6).

2. Adoni-bezek: A Shadow of Kings to Come (see above, p. 27)

In a wider context, Adoni-bezek may be seen as a representative figure of powerful monarchs like the one who "smote the peoples in wrath with unceasing blows, . . . ruled the nations in anger with unrelenting persecution" (Isa. 14:6), "made the earth tremble, . . . shook kingdoms" (v. 16), and boasted "I will make myself like the Most High" (v. 14). The seventy kings of Judg. 1:7 are like the kings in that poem who greet the tyrant from their beds in the underworld saying, "You too have become as weak as we! . . . because you have destroyed your land, you have slain your people" (Isa. 14:10, 20).

Adoni-bezek and the seventy kings bring to mind the NT "thrones . . . dominions . . . principalities . . . authorities" (Col. 1:16) which, though part of God's good order, have turned against God (Eph. 6:12). Jesus, the one "descended from Judah" (Heb. 7:14) and a priest "in the likeness of Melchizedek" (Heb. 7:15), is seen in these writings as the one who will desacralize these powers and then restore them to their proper role in God's good order (Col. 1:16, 20).

In Chinese terms, Adoni-bezek had lost the "mandate of heaven."

> Once a ruler has lost the mandate of heaven, his fall from the height of heaven becomes inevitable. . . . He is immediately demythologized. His true nature is exposed. His vicious acts are displayed before the people. He is reduced to a mere criminal who deserves death. How tragic and miserable is the end of a king, when all aura of kingly glory and divine majesty leaves him! (Choan-Seng Song, *The Compassionate God,* 155)

3. Jerusalem in the Scribe's Time (see above, pp. 28-29)

It is possible to see in this brief note about the temporary cleansing of Jerusalem an echo of the Jerusalem of the Scribe's time, which was greatly in need of cleansing from the "Canaanite" stains of injustice and immorality. Jeremiah was telling "the men of Judah and the inhabitants of Jerusalem" that Jerusalem would be destroyed and burnt with fire if there was no change in the people's evil practices (Jer. 4:3-4; 6:8). Speaking for God, he uttered words which could have been applied to Canaanite Jerusalem: "How long will it be before you are made clean?" (Jer. 13:27).

We may also sense a connection with the folly of Solomon

(1 Kgs. 11:1-8), the "abominations" of Manasseh (2 Kgs. 21:2-16), and the sorry events of the reign of Jehoiakim (2 Kgs. 23:34–24:7), all of which took place in Jerusalem. A century earlier Isaiah had prophesied a time to come "when the LORD shall have washed away the filth of the daughters of Zion and cleansed the bloodstains of Jerusalem from its midst by a spirit of judgment and by a spirit of burning" (Isa. 4:4). The Scribe could have been aware of the evaluation of Jerusalem by Isaiah (Isa. 1:21-23) and Jeremiah (Jer. 7:1-15). From a later perspective, we can relate this incident to Jesus' lament over Jerusalem (Matt. 23:37-38).

Although Josiah's reforms involved a similar cleansing of the city (2 Kgs. 23:4-14), the reform had apparently failed by the time of Jehoiakim. What the "men of Judah" had done at the beginning (Judg. 1:8) needed to be done again.

4. Tyrannical Power: A Recurring Problem (see above, p. 30)

We find the three sons of Anak at Hebron mentioned by name in three different periods of Israelite history. We may think of these as three successive generations of tyrants.

The first generation struck such terror into the hearts of the spies who came to Hebron that the Israelites were frightened into disobedience, and postponed their entry into the Promised Land for forty years (Num. 13:22, 33). Caleb drove the second generation of Anakim out of power (Josh. 15:14), and Joshua himself wiped them out of the hill country of Judah, so that they had to find refuge in Gaza and other cities along the coast (Josh. 11:21). Finally, in the time of the judges, it was necessary for Judah to "defeat" the third generation of tyrants!

Judah's victory over the tyrants was a cleansing action, "as one wipes a dish" (2 Kgs. 21:13). The history of Israel shows clearly that the problem of tyranny and injustice did not disappear with their defeat. In the Scribe's day a new generation of tyrants had arisen: the kings, princes, and priests of Judah (Jer. 1:18-19).

The Scribe's note about the defeat of the three tyrants at Hebron is in some ways parallel to the note about Adoni-bezek and the cleansing of Jerusalem. Adoni-bezek may be seen as a symbol of a desacralized Canaanite kingship, pointing at the same time to the canaanized king, Abimelech (Judg. 9), as well as the wicked kings Manasseh (2 Kgs. 21) and Jehoiakim (2 Kgs. 23:36-37) of Judah. During Jehoiakim's reign the princes seized Jeremiah, beat and imprisoned him (Jer. 37:14-15), asked the king for permission to kill him, and tried to get rid of him by dropping him into the mire of a dry cistern (Jer. 38:4, 6).

5. *Achsah and Judah (see above, p. 32)*

Although we cannot know what was in the mind of the Scribe as he composed this book, it is instructive to compare some of these pictures in Judges with words from Jeremiah. In Achsah we may see an illustration of these words of the LORD about Israel: "I remember the devotion of your youth, your love as a bride" (Jer. 2:2). The terrible fate of the Levite's concubine finds an exact application in Jeremiah's description of "the daughter of Zion gasping for breath, stretching out her hands," and crying out, "'Woe is me! I am fainting before murderers'" (4:31). The callous indifference of the Levite to the fate of his concubine and his subsequent rage at what the men of Gibeah had done (Judg. 19:25, 27-29), contrast with the pain in God's heart reflected in Jeremiah's words: "For the wound of the daughter of my people is my heart wounded, I mourn, and dismay has taken hold on me" (Jer. 8:21; cf. Jer. 14:17; see below, p. 175).

By placing these texts side by side, we may perhaps grasp something of the purpose of the Scribe in telling the ancient stories. He was holding up a mirror for his own times. Originally the people had been as innocent and pious as Achsah (Jer. 2:2). Later many became more like the women in Samson's life (Jer. 3:2, 11). Yet the common people, like the Levite's concubine, were often victims of the powerful (Jer. 8:21–9:1; 14:17).

THE NORTHERN TRIBES
AT RISK

Judges 1:22-36

BEGINNING AT BETHEL (1:22-26)

The function of the first chapter of Judges is, according to Brevard S. Childs, to "mark the beginning of a period of disobedience which stands in sharp contrast to the period which preceded . . . [and] to offer a theological judgment on the nature of disobedient Israel" (*Introduction to the Old Testament as Literature* [Philadelphia: Fortress and London: SCM, 1979], 259). The Bethel incident serves this purpose well, as an introduction to the third part of the prologue in which the Scribe emphasizes the failure of the northern tribes to drive the Canaanites out of power. In sharp contrast to his view of Judah, the Scribe sees Israel's disobedience as concentrated in the northern tribes (see below, p. 52, "Perspectives," no. 1).

The Bethel incident stands at the beginning of this story of the northern tribes as an artful introduction, to suggest that the sin of the house of Israel in the Promised Land began at Bethel. This is emphasized further by the Bochim incident (Judg. 2:1-5) at the end of the prologue. If we accept the suggestion of the LXX that Bochim is to be located at or near Bethel, then Bethel frames the entire account of the northern tribes.

The House of Joseph

The Bethel incident concerns the house of Joseph, meaning the northern tribes (see note below, p. 42). The Scribe has used the expression "the house of Joseph" three times in a way which again frames this section. His emphatic repetition of this phrase in vv. 22-23 at the beginning is balanced by the note at the end that "the hand of the house of Joseph rested heavily" on the Amorites (v. 35).

Judah and Joseph: Two Different Beginnings

When the Scribe wrote the word "also" (Judg. 1:22; the Hebrew expression is emphatic: "they too!"), he put the house of Joseph in parallel with Judah in vv. 2-21. As Judah had gone up against the Canaanites (v. 4), so the house of Joseph "went up" to Bethel (v. 22). As the LORD was "with Judah" (v. 19), so he was with the house of Joseph (v. 22). Yet the beginnings made by Judah and Joseph are presented very differently.

Although the RSV translates "went up *against* Bethel," the Hebrew of v. 22 does not have the word translated "against" as it does in the case of Judah (v. 9). The grammatical structure is the same as that used to describe a pilgrimage to a shrine (Gen. 35:1; Judg. 20:26). It is also used by Hosea, who said scornfully, "Enter not into Gilgal, nor go up to Beth-aven [Bethel]" (Hos. 4:15; cf. Amos 4:4; 5:5). Perhaps the Scribe had something more than a military campaign in mind when he spoke of the movement of the house of Joseph up to Bethel.

Bethel, the Canaanized Shrine City

Bethel was no neutral place name for the Scribe or his readers in the 7th century. It will be necessary to look at other references to the city in order to uncover the meaning of this brief incident in the story of the northern tribes.

The Jacob Traditions. Bethel was formerly a city in the land of Canaan called Luz (Judg. 1:23). By referring to its former identity, the Scribe connects this incident with the Jacob traditions. Jacob gave the Canaanite city its new name, Bethel (Gen. 28:19; 35:15), because God had revealed himself (28:12; 35:6-7) and blessed Jacob there (28:15; 48:3). It was at Luz that God renewed his promise of the land to Jacob's descendants (Gen. 28:13; 35:12; 48:4). Jacob erected a sacred pillar there to worship the God who came to meet him at Bethel (Gen. 28:18; 35:14). The ascent to Bethel by the northern tribes thus could be seen as a claim on the revelation, blessing, and promise of the land which had been made there.

In *the Joshua story* Bethel appears not as an Israelite holy place but as a Canaanite city-state opposed to Israel. Joshua's ambush lay "between Bethel and Ai" (Josh. 8:9, 12) in the same general location as Abraham's altar to the LORD (Gen. 12:8). The men of Bethel joined those of Ai in the unsuccessful resistance to Joshua's forces (Josh. 8:17). The king of Bethel was an enemy defeated by Joshua (Josh. 12:16).

In *the period of the Monarchy,* Bethel the holy place became the center of idolatry. Jeroboam chose it as one of two shrine cities for the location of his golden bull images, which "became a sin" for the northern kingdom (1 Kgs. 12:29-30). Jeroboam offered sacrifices on the altar and appointed nonlevitical priests to serve there (1 Kgs. 12:31-32). A prophetic protest against this idolatrous shrine climaxes with the prediction of the destruction of the altar by Josiah (1 Kgs. 13:32). Amos confronted the priest Amaziah at Bethel, "the king's sanctuary" (Amos 7:10-13). Readers of Judges would recall the words of Amos that Yahweh would "punish the altars of Bethel" (Amos 3:14) with "fire in the house of Joseph . . . for Bethel" (5:6); or the words of Hosea that the "high places of Aven [Bethel], the sin of Israel" would be destroyed (Hos. 10:8; cf. v. 5). With this history in mind, the ascent to Bethel could also be seen as the beginning of the downfall of the northern kingdom.

In the time of the Scribe "the house of Joseph" had already gone into exile in 732 and 722 (2 Kgs. 15:29; 17:6). A northern priest of the line set up by Jeroboam had been brought back from Mesopotamia and installed by the Assyrians at Bethel (2 Kgs. 17:28). Bethel is the one shrine mentioned by name in the historian's record of Josiah's purge of the north. Josiah not only destroyed the altar and shrine at Bethel (2 Kgs. 23:15), but killed its priests, along with those in other northern shrines (vv. 19-20). Jeremiah supported this destruction because Bethel had become a source of false confidence to Israel (Jer. 48:13). These events would have been fresh in the minds of the Scribe's audience.

Readers who knew the sacred origin of the city and its subsequent canaanization in Israel and who remembered its destruction in Josiah's reform would sense here a tragic dimension. They would know, like the readers of a dramatic tragedy, the fateful meaning of the words that "the house of Joseph went up" to canaanized Bethel, almost as on a pilgrimage to a shrine. True, the narrative tells of a victory over the city, which became an Israelite cult center (Judg. 20:18, 26; 21:2). Yet it was this very conquered Canaanite shrine which became the source of Canaanite influence and the way of death that ultimately destroyed the northern kingdom (see above, pp. 15-16, and see below, pp. 52-53; "Perspectives," no. 2).

Luz Rebuilt: Risky Cooperation with the Canaanites

The seemingly inconsequential note at the end of the Bethel incident takes on new dimensions in the light of this discussion. Luz, the Canaanite city, came back to life again "in the land of the Hittites" (see note below) with the help of a friendly house of Joseph. This is perhaps the first hint of the theme developed in subsequent verses by the Scribe, that risky cooperation with the Canaanites was the basic problem of the northern tribes (see below, p. 53, "Perspectives," no. 3).

Note on the House of Joseph

In nine out of the ten occurrences of the phrase "the house of Joseph" in the OT it refers to the northern tribes or the northern kingdom. (The one exception is Josh. 17:17, where the term is limited to Ephraim and Manasseh.) Joshua refers to the territory of Judah "on the south" and that of the house of Joseph "on the north" (Josh. 18:5). Shimei of Benjamin was "the first of all the house of Joseph" to declare loyalty to David after the suppression of Absalom's revolt (2 Sam. 19:20). Solomon put Jeroboam of Ephraim over "all the forced labor of the house of Joseph" (1 Kgs. 11:28). Amos warned "the house of Joseph" of the coming wrath of God (Amos 5:6; cf. 5:15; 6:6; see also Obad. 18). The hope of the prophets after the Exile was for the restoration of both the house of Judah and the house of Joseph (Zech. 10:6; cf. Ezek. 37:16, 19). It is clear that the Scribe is referring to the northern tribes as a whole, rather than to the two sons of Joseph, Ephraim and Manasseh.

Note on "the Land of the Hittites"

The location of the "land of the Hittites" where the man of Bethel rebuilt Luz is not clear. It could be an inclusive description of the whole of the land promised to Joshua (Josh. 1:4). Historical considerations may point to a location north of Canaan in what is now Syria. Against this location we should bear in mind that the expression "to this day" (Judg. 1:26) always refers to a continuing phenomenon in Israel and never to one outside of Israel. Furthermore, the promise to "deal kindly" (Judg. 1:24) with the man of Bethel and with "all his family" (v. 25) implies a friendly relationship which would not suggest any need for the man to flee from the Josephites (Norman K. Gottwald, *The Tribes of Yahweh*, 559-61). Reference to the Hittites in the list of nations among whom the Israelites lived (Judg. 3:5) should help the reader see the possibility that "the land of the Hittites" may have been a description of a part of the land of Canaan, perhaps the hill country (Num. 13:29; Josh. 11:3). In addition to his kinship group (Judg. 1:25), the man of Bethel may even have taken with him a group of Bethelites who were dissatisfied with the rule of its king, to help build the new city of Luz (v. 26).

A LITANY OF LAMENT (1:27-33)

Following the Bethel incident is a sevenfold repetition of the phrase "did not drive out [of power]" (Judg. 1:27, 28, 29, 30, 31, 32, 33) which makes this passage sound like a litany of lament anticipating the demise of the northern tribes (compare the similar refrain, "yet you did not return to me," Amos 4:6, 8, 9, 10, 11). It stands in sharp contrast with the Scribe's approving description of Judah's record in the south. He uses the phrase only once of Judah (Judg. 1:19; see above, pp. 34-35). No excuse is offered in the case of the northern tribes. The melancholy refrain underlines the risky situation of the northern tribes which in the end had proved their undoing. This litany gives added meaning to the weeping at Bochim (see below, pp. 54-57).

The sad retrospect implied in this literary device is related to two other passages. The first is Joshua's farewell warning to all Israel that covenant-breaking and perverse loyalty to other gods would mean the end of their life in the Promised Land (Josh. 23:16). The warning had already come true for the northern tribes in the time of the Scribe (2 Kgs. 15:29; 17:5-6, 23b).

The other relevant passage is the historian's melancholy comment on the destruction of the northern kingdom by Assyria:

And this was so, because the people of Israel had sinned against the LORD their God . . . and had feared other gods and walked in the customs of the nations . . . and in the customs which the kings of Israel had introduced. . . . They went after false idols, and became false, and they followed the nations that were round about them, concerning whom the LORD had commanded them that they should not do like them. (2 Kgs. 17:7-8, 15)

An implied lesson for Judah is discernible here: following the collapse of Josiah's reformation, Judah itself stood in the same risky position as the northern tribes at the beginning.

SHARED POWER IN THE NORTH

In the setting of the 12th cent. B.C.E., Judg. 1:27-33 presents a picture of shared power in the north. The text mentions seventeen city-states whose "inhabitants [rulers]" were too entrenched for the Israelites to dislodge from power (vv. 27, 29, 30, 31, 33). We find three patterns of power sharing (see above, pp. 14, 20).

First pattern: an expanding coalition within an aging imperial power structure (vv. 27-29). The remaining Canaanite city-states in the territory of Ephraim and Manasseh in central Canaan (Bethshean, Taanach, Ibleam, Megiddo, Dor, and Gezer) were part of the former Egyptian communications network which controlled major trade routes. Two roads extended up from the Mediterranean seacoast eastward to the central highlands, the Jordan Valley, and on to the "King's Highway" (Num. 20:17) in Transjordan. On the southern border of Ephraim was the road from Gezer (Judg. 1:29) east to Aijalon (v. 35) and Jerusalem (v. 21). On the northern border of Manasseh was the route from Dor on the coast to Megiddo, Taanach, Ibleam, and Beth-shean (v. 27). Both of these connected on the west with the major trade route from Egypt by way of Gaza (Judg. 1:18) to Joppa, Megiddo (v. 27), and Hazor (4:2) in the north (John F. A. Sawyer, *From Moses to Patmos* [London: SPCK, 1977], 35-36).

The tribes of Ephraim and Manasseh controlled the central hill

country except for the two East-West communication routes from
Gezer to Jerusalem and from Dor to Beth-shean (Judg. 1:27, 29).
These tribes formed "a very broad alliance of extended families,
protective associations, and tribes" composed of the descendants
of Hebrews who had come out of Egypt, plus Canaanite poor or
other victims of the oppressive city-state system who had risen up
against their oppressors and joined the Israelite coalition (Norman K. Gottwald, "Early Israel and the Canaanite Socio-economic
System," 30).

This alliance had taken over the socio-economic, religious, and
military functions of the Canaanite city-states at the village and
tribal levels. In this way they were able to create new and wider
areas of political unity than the fragmented city-state system under
Egyptian domination. This period was thus a preparation for the
later achievement of national unity under the monarchy.

It was also at this time that the Israelite legal tradition, initiated
by Moses, began to develop in the context of extended families,
villages, and tribes. Some ideals of this legal tradition show
distinctive differences from the royal-administrative structures of
the Canaanite city-states:

1. God alone gave the law to the whole people, not just to
the king (Exod. 20:1-2);
2. The law recognizes no class distinctions (Lev. 19:15);
3. The law places the rights of persons above those related to
property (Exod. 22:26-27);
4. Israelites must give sanctuary to fugitives from overbear-
ing power and make them a part of their community (Num.
35:25).

These "polemically deviant ideals" would certainly appeal to
oppressed Canaanites (Marvin L. Chaney, "Ancient Palestinian
Peasant Movements and the Formation of Premonarchic Israel,"
71). Despite the "litany of lament," and the obvious violations of
accepted standards in the stories of the judges, it is important to
recognize the creativity of this period in Israelite history.

*Second Pattern: Self-sufficient villages surrounding Canaanite cit-
ies.* In Zebulun to the west of the Sea of Chinnereth (Galilee),
two Canaanite city-states remained: Kitron and Nahalol (Judg.
1:30). Neither has been identified or located, but Nahalol is

45

probably the same as Nahalal (Josh. 19:15), which was also designated as a levitical city in the days of the Monarchy (Josh. 21:35; see E. John Hamlin, *Inheriting the Land,* 146). In Naphtali (Judg. 1:33) to the north of Zebulun, two more city-states continued to hold power. Their names reflect Canaanite religion: Beth-shemesh means "Temple of the [god] Sun," and Beth-anath, "Temple of [the goddess] Anath."

The location and size of these Canaanite city-states shows that they were dependent on exchange of goods with surrounding territories and other cities. In contrast to this pattern, the Israelites lived in small and largely self-sufficient villages (Carol L. Meyers, "Of Seasons and Soldiers," 52-53). In this way power was shared without obvious conflict, though with great risk, as we note from Judg. 3:5-6.

Third Pattern: Israelites surrounded by Canaanite cities. The Asherites (Judg. 1:31-32) had been present in Canaan long before the arrival of Joshua (Yohanan Aharoni, *The Land of the Bible,* 179), and had not themselves experienced the events of the Exodus liberation or the covenant bonding at Sinai. Reference to Asher dwelling "at the coast of the sea, settling down by his landings . . ." (Judg. 5:17) may indicate that the Asherites served as laborers for the Canaanite sea traders (Roland de Vaux, *The Early History of Israel,* 664, 779).

The Scribe tells us that, in the territory of Asher, seven Canaanite cities retained power (1:31). In no other tribal territory were there this number of cities still controlled by the Canaanites. The probability that Ahlab and Helbah, with identical consonants, are two names for the same site and variant spellings of the Mahalab of Josh. 19:29 (Gus W. Van Beek, "Helbah," *IDB* 2:578) suggests that the number seven is intentional rather than accidental. If we understand the number "seven" in its symbolic meaning of completeness (Marvin H. Pope, "Seven, Seventh, Seventy," *IDB* 4:294-95), we may sense a hidden indication that of all the tribes Asher was at maximum risk. The surprising inclusion of Ahlab north of Tyre and Sidon still further north (a northern border city in Josh. 19:28) only emphasizes the risk of exposure to foreign influences.

Sidon, like Tyre and Byblos, was a center of Canaanite shipping and trade with wide connections in the Mediterranean as well as overland contacts with Mesopotamia (Robert R. Stieglitz, "Long-distance Seafaring in the Ancient Near East," *Biblical Archaeologist* 47 [1984]: 134-42).

We learn from subsequent history that Asher was the channel for both Baalistic corruption and foreign invasion. The Canaanite shrine on Mt. Carmel across the Bay of Haifa from Acco was the focus of Elijah's struggle to purify the northern kingdom of the corrupting influence of Canaanite gods (1 Kgs. 18:20-40). Solomon's barter (1 Kgs. 9:11, 14) made them the first of many exiled groups to be absorbed by other cultures. Tiglath-Pilezer III's campaign route of 733 crossed from Hazor to Acco in Asher (Judg. 1:31; Yohanan Aharoni and Michael Avi-Yonah, *The Macmillan Bible Atlas,* map 147).

AND FINALLY DAN (1:34-36)

An Interrupted Sequence

The geographical sequence of this chapter has been from Judah in the south, to Ephraim and Manasseh, and on to Galilee in the north. This sequence is abruptly interrupted by the mention of the Danites in the south. The cities mentioned in 1:35 are located on the western borders of Judah, Benjamin, and Ephraim. Aijalon and Shaalbim (Shaalabbin) were originally assigned to Dan (Josh. 19:42) but later became a part of Ephraim (Aharoni and Avi-Yonah, *The Macmillan Bible Atlas,* map 73). If Har-heres is another name for Beth-shemesh (Aharoni, *The Land of the Bible,* 236), it was a border town (Josh. 15:10), which later became a part of Judah (Aharoni and Avi-Yonah, *The Macmillan Bible Atlas,* map 73). This apparent mislocation of Dan may be better understood if we keep in mind the perspective of the Scribe, who was writing for readers in the time after the death of King Josiah in 609 B.C.E.

Dan: The Future Northern Border City

The tribe of Dan eventually moved from their assigned location in the south to the city of Dan in the extreme north (Josh. 19:47; Judg. 18; see below, pp. 154-56). With this future perspective, we can see how the northern direction of the listing of tribes in Judg. 1:27-35 was maintained. Dan was the traditional northernmost boundary of "all Israel" as seen at the end of Judges (Judg. 20:1). "From Dan to Beer-sheba" symbolizes the unity of "all Israel" in the days of Samuel (1 Sam. 3:20), David (2 Sam. 3:10; 24:2), Solomon (1 Kgs. 4:25), and Hezekiah (2 Chron. 30:5). Dan was the first of the tribes to be lost to external enemies (1 Kgs. 15:20) and the point of entry for enemy armies threatening Judah (Jer. 4:15; 8:16). Dan could be seen in the days of the Scribe as signifying the northern boundary of the once and future unity of God's people.

Dan: The Idolatrous Shrine City

Dan was long a shrine city and later became an official center of the royal cult, established along with Bethel as a northern rival to Jerusalem after the division of the kingdom in 922. The shrines at Dan and Bethel remained a scandal in Israel as late as Jehu's reform, which ended the dynasty of Omri in 842 (2 Kgs. 10:29). In the days of Jeroboam II people would take oaths by "your God, O Dan" (Amos 8:14 NEB). The unfaithfulness of the northern tribes in contrast to the faithfulness of Judah is emphasized by the fact that the narrative about the northern tribes is bracketed by implied references to Bethel and Dan, the two idolatrous shrine cities (Judg. 1:22-23, 34).

Archaeologists have uncovered an ancient high place (worship center) at Dan, with monumental steps added in the 9th-8th cents. (Jeroboam I's reign?) and an Israelite horned altar south of the steps (Avraham Biran, "Dan [City]," 205). The story of the Danites in Judges ends with the words that they "set up the graven image for themselves" (Judg. 18:30, 31). This surely points forward to the stated reasons for the fall of the northern kingdom, that "they went after false idols, and became false, . . . and made for themselves molten images of two calves" (2 Kgs. 17:15-16). The sequence in Judg. 1 of which Dan forms the climax is, then, a series of compromises with Canaanite gods. Geography is secondary to theology from this perspective.

THE AMORITES: FIRST OPPRESSORS (1:34-36)

The Amorites are said to have "pressed" the Danites back into the hill country. The same Hebrew word *(lahats)* is more usually translated as "oppress." This brief notice is thus an arrow put here by the Scribe pointing to all the future oppressors of Israel (Judg. 2:18; 4:3; 6:9; 10:12; 1 Sam. 10:18).

The Scribe is using the term "Amorites" in an ethical or theological, rather than in an historical or ethnic, sense (see note below). We read of "the iniquity of the Amorites" (Gen. 15:16) and the "gods of the Amorites, in whose land you dwell" (Josh. 24:15; Judg. 6:10), which were constant temptations to the Israelites (E. John Hamlin, "Nations," 520-21). Two kings, Ahab of Israel (1 Kgs. 21:26) and Manasseh of Judah (2 Kgs. 21:11), are said to have followed the example of the Amorites in idolatry and wickedness.

Note on the Amorites

The Amorites, mentioned three times for emphasis in Judg. 1:34-36, are, like Dan, something of a surprise at the end of this chapter in which the term "Canaanite" predominates (see above, p. 14). They are definitely not the Amorites of Transjordan (Judg. 10:8; 11:19, 21) or the western highland Amorites (Num. 13:29; Josh. 5:1), who formed offensive coalitions against Joshua (Josh. 10:5; 11:3). In Judg. 1:34-35 we find them on the coastal plain, or perhaps in the Shephelah lowlands, preventing the establishment of Dan in their assigned territory, as the Philistines will do in the Samson stories (Judg. 13:1). They may be related to "the inhabitants of the plain," who resisted Judah's expansion with their iron chariots (Judg. 1:19), or the "pre-Philistines" of Shamgar's time (see below, pp. 79-80). In v. 36 they are on Israel's southern border in the extreme south (cf. Num. 34:3-4). According to one historian, the term " 'Amorite' has no historical or ethnic significance at all" in the Bible (de Vaux, *The Early History of Israel*, 133).

FORCED LABOR: THE WAY OF CANAAN
(1:28, 30, 33, 35)

There are four references to forced labor (Heb. *mas*) in Judg. 1:22-31. They name "the house of Joseph" (v. 35), "Israel" (v. 28, meaning the northern tribes as in Josh. 17:13), Zebulun (Judg. 1:30), and Naphtali (v. 33; cf. Josh. 16:10, where Ephraim is mentioned) as having impressed the Canaanites/Amorites into forced labor gangs. The reader of Judges is bound to ask why the Scribe inserts these notes in the narrative about the northern tribes and omits any reference to forced labor in Judah. Here are some possible answers:

1. The Scribe is referring to actual historical situations other-wise unattested in the premonarchical period, but he overlooks forced labor in Judah because of his pro-Judah point of view.

2. The Scribe is referring to actual historical situations in the northern kingdom ("house of Joseph," Judg. 1:35), which would help to explain the fact that these kingdoms had fallen to the Assyrians in 732 and 721.

3. The Scribe is using this example of covenant violation to illustrate the difference between Judah's radical discontinuity with Canaanite "abominable practices" and the northern tribes' compromises with Canaanite values. "The house of Joseph" had, in his theological reconstruction, been the first to practice this kind of oppression of the foreigner.

Note on Forced Labor

Forced Labor in Egypt. According to the Exodus tradition, a powerful Egyptian emperor had "set taskmasters [literally, foremen of forced labor gangs] over them to afflict them with heavy burdens" (Exod. 1:11). He gave them no rest from their burdens (Exod. 5:4-5) until their spirit was broken (6:9). Moses was moved to anger when he saw the burden of forced labor (Exod. 2:11). God saw "the oppression with which the Egyptians oppress them" (Exod. 3:9) and showed his power by bringing them out from under the burden of the Egyptians (6:6-7). In later years priests reminded the Israelites that God had "broken the bars of your yoke and made you walk erect" (Lev. 26:13). The liberated should be liberators, not oppressors.

Forced Labor in Canaan. It is likely that members of the northern tribes who had not been in Egypt, but joined the covenant league in the time of Joshua, had been part of forced labor gangs, as we see from the words in the song of Jacob that "Issachar . . . became a slave at forced labor" (Gen. 49:14-15). Issachar was probably

in the Galilee region two centuries before the Exodus from Egypt
(de Vaux, *The Early History of Israel,* 664). They and many other
oppressed people in Canaan would have welcomed the liberation
brought by Joshua. Their village economy would have had no
place for forced labor.

Israel Before the Monarchy. There is no evidence for the practice of
forced labor in Israel before the Monarchy (Anson F. Rainey, "Compulsory Labor Gangs in Ancient Israel," 191-202; Gottwald, *The
Tribes of Yahweh,* 168-69; Roland de Vaux, *Ancient Israel,* 141). In
fact, Samuel warned those who demanded to have a king "like all the
nations" that forced labor was one of the ways of Canaanite kings
(1 Sam 8:11-17; cf. Isa. 31:8). Forced labor could have been one
meaning of the "fire . . . out of the bramble" of Jotham's fable, which
was critical of Abimelech's Canaanite style kingship (Judg. 9:15).
The four references to forced labor in the Scribe's introductory
description of the northern tribes in all likelihood show his perspective of several centuries after the time of the judges themselves.

When Israel Grew Strong. Forced labor became a part of Israelite
society with the coming of the monarchy. David first imposed it
on the Ammonites (2 Sam. 12:31) and appointed an official in
charge of these forced labor gangs (20:24). With Solomon, forced
labor became a national institution. Adoram (or Adoniram),
probably a Phoenician (de Vaux, *Ancient Israel,* 129, 142), was
his minister of forced labor (1 Kgs. 4:6; 5:14). Under him were
3300 officers to supervise the gangs who worked on Solomon's
ambitious building projects in Jerusalem (1 Kgs. 7:1-12; 9:15)
and the fortress cities of Hazor, Megiddo, Gezer, Lower Beth-
horon, Baalath, and Tamar (9:15, 17-19). The royal program
needed levies *(mas)* of thousands of workers in the forests of
Lebanon (1 Kgs. 5:14) and the stone quarries around Jerusalem
(vv. 15-18).

The obvious source of this cheap labor was the population of
the newly conquered territories which had not previously been
incorporated into Israelite borders (1 Kgs. 9:20-21). When this
supply proved to be inadequate, it became necessary to involve
the Israelite population itself as members of the labor gangs
(1 Kgs. 5:13). Even this did not prevent such enormous cost
overruns that Solomon had to pay his debts by ceding territory
from the tribe of Asher to Tyre (1 Kgs. 9:10-11).

Forced Labor: A Fatal Weakness. The use of forced labor gangs proved to be the undoing of Solomon's kingdom. The northern tribes so resented it that they stoned Adoram/Adoniram to death, separated themselves from the kingdom, and made Jeroboam, a former overseer of forced labor of "the house of Joseph" (1 Kgs. 11:28), king of the northern kingdom (12:16-20). The principle of "one law for the sojourner and for the native" (Lev. 24:22; cf. Num. 15:29; Josh. 20:9) was a warning that oppression of the foreigner would lead to oppression of the citizen.

Jeremiah's "social criticism" (Walter Brueggemann, "Unity and Dynamic in the Isaiah Tradition," *Journal for the Study of the Old Testament* 29 [1984]: 92) of Jeroboam II's "oppression and violence" (Jer. 22:13, 17) provides an appropriate setting for the Scribe's interest in forced labor.

PERSPECTIVES

1. Judah and the Northern Tribes (see above, p. 39)

The Scribe's retrospective portrayal of Judah in such idealistic terms must be seen against the Judah of the time of the Scribe and Jeremiah. In Jeremiah's view, the northern tribes had gone astray first. It was only after Judah imitated "faithless Israel" that they began to follow the Canaanite way of death as "false Judah" (Jer. 3:6-11). Jeremiah did not give up hope that a "righteous Branch" of David's line would come in the future to "deal wisely, and . . . execute justice and righteousness in the land" (23:5).

Placing these texts together will give some perspective on particular nations, classes, or parties (especially one's own!) which may believe that they have a "messianic" role in a given moment of history, like that assumed by the Scribe for Judah. It is quite possible for such a nation, class, or party to become corrupt like "false Judah."

2. The Ambiguity of Religious Institutions (see above, pp. 41-42)

The complex history of Bethel illustrates the ambiguity of religious centers and institutions. They may be a source of inspiration and true teaching about God at one time and of corruption at another.

At its best Israelite worship transformed Canaanite ideas and institutions, such as festivals and sacrifice, to make them expressions of the worship of Yahweh. At Bethel the opposite took place. Canaanite practices and ideas turned the people away from the true God. In our time the influence of civic religion can turn churches into nationalistic shrines. Ideology from powerful interests clothed in sermons on television or radio can corrupt the witness of Christians.

3. Risky Cooperation (see above, p. 42)

The risk involved in a life shared with the Canaanites was that the northern tribes would learn the "Canaanite way of death" (see above, pp. 15-16). God's will was that the Canaanites and other peoples should learn from Israel the way of life (Deut. 4:6; Isa. 2:2-3; Jer. 12:16). Christians are always in this situation of "risky cooperation." Some parents will take their children out of the temptations of modern life. Others will try to equip their children at home and in church to be a "light to the nations." Some Christian groups will expel from membership anyone who marries someone of another religious belief. Others will encourage the Christian partner to be a witness to the life-giving Gospel in the marriage relationship. A person in business is always facing the challenge of living as a Christian in the often immoral life of the business world of which he or she is a part. The same is true for anyone in government or any other kind of public life.

ISRAEL'S LAMENT
Judges 2:1-5

A KEY TO JUDGES

This episode pictures all "the people of Israel," gathered together as in 1:1. This time, however, instead of making confident inquiry about how to begin the campaigns in Canaan, they are weeping before the angel of Yahweh at Bochim (probably at or near Bethel). The phrase "all the people of Israel" occurs only in Judg. 2:4 and 20:26, giving the impression of careful design by the Scribe. (What would seem to be an exception in 10:8 refers only to Israelites living east of the Jordan.) Indeed, Israel's lament in the prologue is repeated with triple intensity in the epilogue when, once again, "the people of Israel" weep bitterly before Yahweh at Bethel (20:23, 26; 21:2).

Sounds of weeping thus enclose the entire book of Judges. Echoes of lament are heard throughout the book of Judges in Israel's repeated cries for help (3:15, etc.) and their remorseful confession, "we have sinned" (10:15). These cries follow acts of unfaithfulness (3:7, 12, etc.) and resultant oppression (3:12-14, etc.). The tears of Jephthah's daughter and "the daughters of Israel" (11:37-38, 40) also resonate with the laments of the prologue and epilogue.

The sounds of lament at Bochim reverberate in the Hebrew Scriptures, whether in the wilderness (Num. 11:4; 14:1), at the ominous approach of an enemy (1 Sam. 11:4), in a time of defeat (1 Sam. 30:4), or because of the total devastation of land and society (Isa. 33:7-9). At Bochim we anticipate the "lamentation and bitter weeping" of Rachel, the ancestress of the northern kingdom, over the loss of her people in the exiles of 732 and 721 (Jer. 31:15). We may catch overtones of Zion's sleepless sobbing over the destruction of temple, city, and nation (Lam. 1:2, 16; see below, p. 57, "Perspectives," no. 1).

RITUALIZED WEEPING

Some scholars have suggested that Bochim was the Canaanite name of a threshing floor near Bethel where ceremonial weeping took place each year (Flemming F. Hvidberg, *Weeping and Laughter in the Old Testament*, 105-6). The name, which means "weepers," seems to support this interpretation of Bochim as a place of Canaanite ritualized weeping. This kind of weeping was a formalized expression of deep human anxiety at harvest time, which marked the seasonal end of the earth's fertility. Behind the tears was the question: Will there be another growing season, or is this the end? The loss of fertility during the dry season, which brought fear of death to human society, was symbolized by belief in the death of Baal.

According to Israelite faith, the change of seasons was part of God's faithfulness (Gen. 8:22). Natural disasters were occasions to return to God (Amos 4:6-10; Joel 2:12-13). Yet in the Scribe's time a similar kind of ritualized weeping was being practiced in Judah. During the reign of Zedekiah (597-587), and without doubt in the reign of Jehoiakim as well (609-598), women used to weep for Tammuz (a Babylonian counterpart of Baal) in the Jerusalem temple (Ezek. 8:14). They would make cakes for the Canaanite goddess Anat, "the queen of heaven" (Jer. 7:18; 44:19), and join her in weeping on the hill shrines around Jerusalem for her dead husband Baal (Jer. 3:21; cf. 9:10).

COVENANT WEEPING

The Israelites gave Bochim a new meaning (Judg. 2:5) which was related to covenant disobedience (v. 2) and its consequences (v. 3).

The Angel of the LORD. A primary difference from Canaanite ritualized weeping is seen in the one who prompted Israel to weep: the "angel [messenger] of Yahweh." This particular designation refers to the "executive of the covenant of grace" (Gerhard von Rad, "ἄγγελος," *TDNT* 1:78). This angel brings Covenant Teaching (Judg. 2:1-2) and mediates covenantal grace (Judg. 2:1; cf.

55

6:12; 13:3; Exod. 3:2) and judgment (Judg. 2:3; cf. 5:23; 2 Sam. 24:16). He fights against Israel's enemies (Exod. 33:2), guides Israel along the way (Exod. 23:23), suffers with, redeems, and carries his people (Isa. 63:9).

Bearing Yahweh's name (Exod. 23:21), he speaks God's words and does God's command. At times he is indistinguishable from Yahweh himself (note the change in subject from the angel to Yahweh in Judg. 6:12, 14, etc). In sum, *this angel is Yahweh's personalized, effective presence, visible or invisible, at any given time and place.*

Weeping for what? Three different reasons for tears may be seen in this situation. The first is *frustration over "Paradise Lost."* A loss of control due to human weakness and moral perverseness seems to be a permanent part of Israel's history as seen in Judges. The Promised Land "flowing with milk and honey" (Exod. 3:8) appears at Bochim, not as a paradise of continual life under God's blessing, but as a place of testing where the powers of death as well as life are always present, where human adversaries remain to oppress, and where culture gods persist as snares (Judg. 2:3).

The second reason for weeping is *a deep anxiety about coming troubles.* With this kind of a beginning, who would not have anxious thoughts about the future? Those who read or heard about this incident would have a knowledge of the final tragic events of the northern kingdom and the peril of Judah in the time of the Scribe. There is a similarity to the tears of Elisha (2 Kgs. 8:11-12), Isaiah (Isa. 22:4), and Jeremiah (Jer. 9:1; 13:17; 14:17). Jeremiah called on his own people to join him in lament (Jer. 9:10-11; 25:34-38) over the imminent ruin of Zion (9:19).

A repentant appeal to God's grace is a third element in Israel's grieving at Bochim. It was a self-humbling before Yahweh in the faith that a new beginning would be possible (Deut. 30:1-10). Each new savior-judge sent by Yahweh meant a chance to begin again. An interesting parallel is King Josiah's weeping over God's word that Jerusalem and its inhabitants "should become a desolation and a curse" (2 Kgs. 22:19). Josiah not only showed penitence but also attempted to reverse the covenant curse by a covenant renewal ceremony and a cleansing of the land (2 Kgs. 23:1-25; see below, p. 57, "Perspectives," no. 2).

2:1-5   ISRAEL'S LAMENT

PERSPECTIVES

1. Weeping in the New Testament (see above, pp. 54-55)

Echoes of Bochim are found in the NT. Jesus' tears over the
coming destruction of Jerusalem (Luke 19:41; cf. Heb. 5:7)
remind us of those of Isaiah and Jeremiah. Like Jeremiah, Jesus
urges the women of Jerusalem to weep not for him but for
themselves (Luke 23:28). Peter's bitter weeping over his own
betrayal of his LORD (Luke 22:62) expresses both frustration and
anxiety as at Bochim. Likewise, Paul weeps over those who have
become enemies of Christ by their surrender to the cultural values
of their time (Phil. 3:18-19; cf. 2 Cor. 2:4).

2. Covenant Weeping Today (see above, p. 56)

Covenant weeping at Bochim is relevant to our own time in
history. We may grieve over the danger of national ruin (as in Amos
6) or personal disaster (as in Jer. 9:1). We may share the earth's
mourning brought on by violations of the covenant (as in Hos.
4:1-3; cf. Jer 4:23-26), because we realize the possibility of a
totally polluted earth or nuclear winter. Whatever the occasion, the
permanent elements of covenant weeping persist: frustration when
things get out of control, deep anxiety in a frightening world,
humble repentance, and determination to return to covenant
faithfulness.

THEOLOGY OF SIN
AND GRACE
Judges 2:6–3:6

The tears of frustration, anxiety, and petition (Judg. 2:1-5) which close the prologue lead on to this theological essay which gives the Scribe's key to the proper understanding of the stories to follow. In his view, the key factors in the early period—and indeed all later periods—of Israelite history were (1) Israel's faithlessness, (2) God's constructive anger, and (3) God's timely grace. This essay was intended for the listening community in Judah during the darkening years before the end of Jerusalem and Judah in 587 B.C.E. Readers in our day can gain much from his words.

THE MESSAGE IN THE STRUCTURE

The essay is carefully structured in the form of two statements about the post-Joshua generations (A, A'), which enclose two parallel sequences of sin and grace (B-C-D-E-D, B'-C'-D').

A. Two generations contrasted (2:6-10)
  B. The evil deeds of the post-Joshua generation (vv. 11-13)
    C. God's anger: enemy attacks, "sore straits" (vv. 14-15)
      D. God's grace: savior-judges (v. 16)
        E. Persistent unfaithfulness (v. 17)
      D. God's grace: support for the judges out of pity (v. 18)
  B'. More and worse evil deeds (v. 19)
    C'. God's anger: leaving the nations in place (vv. 20-21)
      D'. God's grace: testing his people (vv. 22-23)
A'. The succeeding generations (3:1-6) being trained (vv. 1-2) and tested (v. 4) among the nations and their gods.

TWO GENERATIONS

As the Scribe has done before, he signals the focus of his message by the use of the same word at the beginning (A) and end (A') of his essay. The word "generation" occurs twice in 2:10 and once in plural form in 3:2. Joshua's generation had "served the LORD" (2:7) and "obeyed the commandments of the LORD" (v. 17). The listening community may have been reminded of the good kings, Hezekiah (715-687) and Josiah (640-609), who "did what was right in the eyes of the LORD" (2 Kgs. 18:3; 22:2). This was "the generation of the upright" (Ps. 112:2) "who seek" the LORD (24:6).

In dramatic contrast the post-Joshua generation, who "did not know the LORD" (Judg. 2:10; cf. Gal. 4:8), did evil, served and prostrated themselves before the Canaanite culture gods, and followed their way of death (Judg. 2:11, 12, 13, 17, 19; 3:6).

As the earliest examples of a perennial problem in Israel, they would fit the description of the "perverse generation" (Deut. 32:20), who roused God's anger by their "abominable practices" and their worship of demonic powers (vv. 5, 15-20). They were like the Israelites in Isaiah's time who, lacking knowledge of the LORD, were "offspring of evildoers . . . who deal corruptly" (Isa. 1:3-4). The two most obvious representatives of this "stubborn and rebellious generation" (Ps. 78:8) in the time of the Scribe would have been Hezekiah's son Manasseh and Josiah's son Jehoiakim, both of whom "did what was evil in the sight of the LORD" (2 Kgs. 21:2; 23:37).

The post-Joshua generation is a paradigm not only for Israel's history but for every age. Jesus called his contemporaries "an evil and adulterous generation" (Matt. 12:39; cf. 17:17), while Paul told his fellow Christians that they were living in the midst of "a crooked and perverse generation" (Phil. 2:15; cf. Deut. 32:5).

A DOUBLE SEQUENCE OF SIN AND GRACE

In the first sequence (B-C-D-E-D), the evil deeds of the generation after Joshua (B) stir God to anger, which results in oppression by "their enemies round about" (C). God is then moved by their suffering to send a "judge" to deliver them, not only from their enemies but from their own unfaithfulness. The structure of 2:16-18 (D-E-D) shows God's grace like the arms of a mother or father surrounding wayward Israel even when they continue in their sin. The best comment is by Paul: "Where sin increased, grace abounded all the more" (Rom. 5:20).

The second sequence begins with the people behaving "worse than their fathers" (B'), in accordance with the Scribe's view of the deteriorating situation of Israel in the course of the book of Judges. God's anger brings its inevitable consequences again (C'), but this time it is tempered with patience (D'), indicating a long drawn out process seen to be at work in Israel's history. The peoples living in Canaan are here given a positive role in the maturing of Israel.

GOD'S CALCULATED RISK

The Scribe shared the view that, as in the case of the garden of Eden (Gen. 2:1-17), so in the Promised Land, God knew in advance (Deut. 31:16, 20-21) the risk he was taking in placing his people in the "land flowing with milk and honey" (Deut. 6:3). The Deuteronomic Moses also knew this (Deut. 31:27-29), as did Joshua (Josh. 24:19-20). Inevitably the Promised Land would be an arena for testing covenant faithfulness in concrete situations (Judg. 2:22; 3:4; cf. Exod. 20:20; Deut. 8:2; 13:3). They would also gain skills and courage for the unremitting struggle ("war," Judg. 3:2) against the powers of death and destruction (Deut. 6:14) disguised as benefactors of life (Hos. 2:5).

ISRAEL'S MISSION IDENTITY (see above, p. 17)

The background for this calculated risk lies in God's wider horizon which, from the days of Noah (Gen. 9:19; 10:32), included "all the peoples that are on the face of the earth" as the context for his choice of Israel (Deut. 7:6; 14:2; cf. Gen. 12:3; Amos 3:2; Horst Seebass, "bahar [bachar]," *TDOT* 2:83). This universal dimension shows that Israel's *disciplined holiness* (Lev. 18:3-5; 19:2; cf. Deut. 18:9) was to preserve their mission identity among the nations. Israel should be a model of "a wise and understanding people" (Deut. 4:6-8), so that the nations could learn from them the ways that lead to life (Jer. 12:16). In this perspective, the testing and training of Israel while dwelling among the nations (Judg. 3:5) were *for the sake of the nations* (cf. Isa. 42:6-7; 49:6).

GOD'S CONSTRUCTIVE ANGER (C, C'. 2:14-15, 20-21)

The Scribe pictures God's anger not as irrational or impetuous, but rather as educative and reformative, designed to bring Israel back to the covenant way of life and their mission identity. In the perspective of God's time, his anger is "but for a moment" (Ps. 30:5; cf. Ps. 103:9).

God's anger is kindled by things that happen within Israel, related to their "going after other gods" (B, B'). Isaiah's poem on divine anger (Isa. 5:8-30; 9:8–10:4) helps us to get a more specific idea of these things: land-grabbing from the poor (Isa. 5:8), self-indulgent neglect of the public good (vv. 11-12), perversion of values for the benefit of the powerful (vv. 20-21), bribery in the courts (v. 23), pride and arrogance of the wealthy in their luxurious homes (9:9-10), wickedness in word and deed (v. 17), fierce competition for limited resources with no regard for fellow humans (vv. 19-20), unjust laws rigged to benefit the rich and rob from the poor (10:1-2; see above, pp. 15-16).

In this perspective from the latter days of Israel's history, the evil deeds which stir God's wrath are acts of injustice within a canaanized Israel (cf. Exod. 22:21-24; Mic. 2:2-3).

A TIMELY GRACE

A divine re-evaluation of plans in the light of human actions of faith or unfaith is discernible in the Hebrew word translated "moved to pity" (Judg. 2:18). In every other case (except Ps. 90:13, "have pity"), this word, when describing God's inner thoughts and plans, is translated as "relent" (e.g., Ps. 106:45), "repent" (e.g., Amos 7:3, 6), or "be sorry" (Gen. 6:6-7). Such a re-evaluation could result in a change from wrath to grace (Jer. 18:8), or from grace to wrath (v. 10). As in the incident of the golden calf (Exod. 32:14) or the destruction of Jerusalem (Jer. 42:10), there comes a time when God says "it is enough" (2 Sam. 24:16). Then, at the right time (Gal. 4:4), God intervenes to transform society and begin the re-creation of the world (for a time) through his agents of salvation. Although the timing is God's alone, those with faith ask "Who knows?" whether this is the time for God to "turn and repent" of the severe judgment previously announced (Joel 2:13-14; Jonah 3:9-10; 4:2).

GOD'S AGENTS OF SALVATION

When the sequence of sin and judgment runs its course (cf. Ps. 106:40-43), God acts by sending agents of salvation (D) to save the people in their "sore straits." By the use of the words "groaning" and "oppress" (Judg. 2:18), the Scribe suggests that *each deliverance is a new Exodus* (cf. Exod. 2:24; 3:7, 9; 6:5). His use of the term "raise up" (Judg. 2:16, 18) may indicate that, in his view, the judges were periodic fulfillments of God's promise to "raise up for them a prophet" like Moses (Deut. 18:18). We get the same idea by placing the command "him you shall *heed*" (Deut. 18:15; cf. v. 19) alongside the comment that "they did not *listen* [using the same Hebrew word] to their judges" (Judg. 2:17).

The function of the judges, according to the Scribe, is to "rescue" God's oppressed people from "marauding bands" and to "keep them safe" from enemy power (Judg. 2:16, 18 NEB) during the lifetime of a particular judge (v. 19). The Hebrew verb *shaphat,* usually translated as "judge," may also mean "deliver" (2 Sam. 18:19, 31).

The negative comment that "they did not listen" (Judg. 2:17) implies a teaching (Deut. 18:18) or a ruling (Exod. 18:21-22) function for the judge. As "executive officer" of the tribal league, the judge would preside over intertribal councils and exercise judicial, military, and cultic functions (Frank M. Cross, *Canaanite Myth and Hebrew Epic*, 219n.3). The parallel statement that the people "transgressed my covenant which I commanded their fathers" (Judg. 2:20) suggests a general function of restoring and maintaining the covenant in the daily life of the society (Johannes Pedersen, *Israel, Its Life and Culture* I-II:348-50), giving justice to the poor (cf. Isa. 11:4), judging the people "with righteous judgment," without partiality or bribe, following "justice, and only justice," in the land (Deut. 16:18-20; cf. Ps. 82:3-4). A righteous judge would oppose those who "judge not with justice the cause of the fatherless, to make it prosper, and . . . do not defend the rights of the needy" (Jer. 5:28; cf. Isa. 1:17; Ps. 82:2). God's agents of salvation would bring not only "rest" from enemies (Judg. 3:11; cf. Deut. 12:10; Josh. 23:1; 1 Kgs. 8:56), but life and "length of days" (Deut. 30:20) on the land in their own time.

PART II
THE DRAMATIC NARRATIVES: TWELVE LIBERATOR JUDGES

Judges 3:7–16:31

OTHNIEL, THE MODEL JUDGE
Judges 3:7-11

The Scribe begins his series of dramatic narratives of the judges with a cameo or miniature picture of this model judge, in five brief verses.

THE IMPERIAL OPPRESSOR

Twice-wicked Cushan

Readers today are left to guess about the identity of Israel's first oppressor, mentioned four times. The Scribe has obscured historical details by giving him a nickname: "Twice-wicked Cushan" (Cushan-rishathaim), something like the term "that wicked woman," used to describe Queen Athaliah as the very embodiment of wickedness (2 Chron. 24:7). The vague title "king of Mesopotamia" is equally obscure. We can be sure that during the reign of Jehoiakim (609-597 B.C.E.) it would have evoked bitter memories of Assyrian aggression in the north more than a century earlier (2 Kgs. 17:3-6) and deep anxiety over Babylonian expansion after the death of Josiah in 609 (2 Kgs. 23:29-30) and the Babylonian victory over Egypt at Carchemish in 605 (Jer. 46:2). Perhaps we could compare this symbolic name to Ezekiel's "Gog, chief prince of Meshech and Tubal" (Ezek. 38:3).

Note on the Identity of Cushan

Habakkuk 3:7 associates Cushan with Midian rather than Mesopotamia. Scholars have proposed identifying Cushan-rishathaim as a Cushite (Ethiopian), an Edomite, a Syrian, a Kassite from Babylonia, or a powerful king from Upper Mesopotamia named

Irsu, who invaded Egypt before 1200 B.C.E. (Charles F. Kraft, "Cushan-rishathaim," *IDB* 1:751; cf. Abraham Malamat, "The Egyptian Decline in Canaan and the Sea-Peoples," 26-27, for arguments in favor of Irsu). The problem is that none of these is ever known to have invaded Israel or dominated it for a period of years. The Scribe was not interested in giving his readers historical details.

Disintegration and Disaster in Israel

The name "Israel" appears six times in these verses, showing us a five-step descent into social disintegration and disaster. (1) First, they "did what was evil," violating the covenant way of life (see above, pp. 15-16; cf. Jer. 7:9). (2) This is followed by "forgetting the LORD their God" (the only use of this verb in Judges; it will later be replaced by the stronger word "forsake," Judg. 10:10, 13). In the words of Jeremiah this made the land "a horror" (Jer. 18:15-16; cf. Jer. 2:32; 3:21). (3) The third step is "serving" the gods of Canaan, meaning to love, seek, and follow after these powers of death (cf. Jer. 8:2). (4) God, in his "constructive anger," "sells" (i.e., gives) them entirely into the power of the cruel invader (cf. Judg. 4:2; 10:7; Deut. 32:30). The meaning of this kind of invasion is vividly portrayed by Jeremiah (cf. Jer. 6:1-8). (5) They are compelled to serve the oppressor. The state of the oppressed is described elsewhere as being "in hunger and thirst, in nakedness, and in want of all things," with "a yoke of iron" around their necks (Deut. 28:48).

GOD'S DELIVERER

We have already met Othniel as Caleb's loyal nephew, junior officer, and son-in-law, and as the thoughtful husband of an *Israelite* wife (cf. Judg. 3:6; see above, pp. 31-33). As the only judge from the tribe of Judah, Othniel could symbolize for the Scribe and his readers a future deliverer from Judah who would "reign as king and deal wisely, and . . . execute justice and righteousness in the land" (Jer. 23:5). The contrast with Samson, the last judge, serves to highlight the ideal character of Othniel.

Othniel is identified not primarily by his name (mentioned only twice), but by the verbs which show his saving actions. The comprehensive verb "deliver" is clarified by two following verbs. First, he "judged" Israel (see above, pp. 62-63), bringing about an internal reform. Second, he "went out to war" to win the victory over the oppressor with the active intervention of Yahweh.

LIBERATION

The word "LORD" (Yahweh) appears seven times in these verses. Three of the seven draw our attention: "the sight of the LORD," showing God as the moral governor of the universe (cf. Ps. 11:4; 33:13-15) who sets standards for human behavior; "the anger of the LORD," showing involvement in and response to the human situation (see above, p. 61); and "the Spirit of the LORD," showing personal support of his chosen servant to bring internal chaos and external oppression under control.

The turning point comes when, after eight years, the people cry out to Yahweh from their distress with penitent hearts (as at Bochim). This action, in addition to that of the "deliverer," achieved "rest" for the land for forty years. In the words of Deuteronomy, they had—for one generation—chosen life (Deut. 30:16, 19). To use the words of Paul, they were "being saved" (1 Cor. 1:18).

Note on the Length of Periods of Oppression

In the eyes of the Scribe, the length of the oppression grows with each judge. From one perspective this represents the time needed for Israel to repent and cry to Yahweh. In the case of Othniel, the period is only eight years. In later instances this return to God will take much longer—eighteen (Judg. 3:14; 10:8), twenty (4:3), or forty (13:1) years. The seven-year period preceding the call of Gideon recorded in 6:1 seems to begin a new cycle of deterioration.

EHUD,
THE HANDICAPPED JUDGE
Judges 3:12-30

THE COLONIAL OPPRESSOR

Eglon King of Moab

The Little Fat Bull. "Eglon" means "little bull calf" (cf. David's wife Eglah, whose name means "heifer"; 2 Sam. 3:5). If we take into consideration the remark that Eglon was "a very fat man" (Judg. 3:17), we get the satirical epithet "little fat bull," something like the modern term "fat cat." In this well-told story this ridiculous, obese, pleasure-loving, gullible king is the humorous foil for the crafty, agile but handicapped hero Ehud. It is the king's very fatness that receives the fatal blow (v. 22). As in Pharaoh's dream, "the gaunt and thin" Ehud destroyed "the sleek and fat" Eglon (Gen. 41:4).

The Prosperous Foreign King. Eglon massed a Moabite army with Ammonite and Amalekite mercenaries at the ford of the Jordan River to defeat an inferior Benjaminite militia. He then established a base at Jericho ("city of Palms") from which to project his power along the communication route to Gezer and the seacoast (see above, p. 44, and below, pp. 81-82, 92). To this end, he imposed an annual tribute for eighteen years on the backs of the Benjaminites (Judg. 3:14). Eglon, who grew fat on the tribute, was like the imperialist invader described by Habakkuk who lived "in luxury" (literally, "fat") with rich food taken from conquered peoples (Hab. 1:16); or the rich Jerusalemites who grew "fat and sleek" on their ill-gotten riches extorted from the poor (Jer. 5:26-28); or the prosperous wicked whose "bodies are sound [fat] and sleek," while "their eyes swell out with fatness; . . . always at ease, they increase in riches," but in fact God sets them in "slippery

70

places," and makes them "fall to ruin . . . in a moment, swept away utterly by terrors" (Ps. 73:4, 7, 12, 18-19). Eglon is an example of a wealthy oppressor whose moment had come (see above, pp. 35-36, "Perspectives," no. 2).

The Ruler who Used Religion to Justify Expansionist Policies. The name Eglon was probably an abbreviation of a personal name compounded with Chemosh, the name of the Moabite national god (Num. 21:29). The full name may have been "Young Bull of Chemosh" (for other Moabite compound names, see Edward D. Grohman, "Moab," *IDB* 3:418). A stone carved bas-relief of the storm god Hadad (Baal) standing on the back of a young bull (G. Ernest Wright, *Biblical Archaeology* [Philadelphia: Westminster, 1957], 147; William F. Albright, *Yahweh and the Gods of Canaan,* 197-98) suggests that Eglon's name would place him in a particularly close relationship with Chemosh, as the god's steed or servant.

The Moabite king Mesha, three centuries after Eglon (2 Kgs. 3:4), claimed to be acting under Chemosh's command when he captured Nebo from the Israelites and slaughtered "seven thousand men, boys, women, girls, and female slaves" (Moabite Stone, lines 14-17; Ronald J. Williams, "Moabite Stone," *IDB* 3:420). No doubt Eglon believed he was acting under Chemosh's orders to invade and impose tribute on Benjamin (see below, pp. 75-76, "Perspectives," no. 1).

This brings us to "the sculptured stones" (Judg. 3:19, 26). In every other instance the Hebrew word is translated as "graven images," "images," or "idols" (e.g., Deut. 7:5; Hos. 11:2). Most probably these monuments were freestanding images of Chemosh and other Moabite gods who were thought to be witnesses of a vassal treaty imposed on Benjamin by Moab (John Gray, *Joshua, Judges, Ruth,* 251; Robert G. Boling, *Judges,* 86). They would also be a bitter reminder of the fact that, by virtue of military might, this was Chemosh's land rather than Yahweh's land (Josh. 22:19). In Ehud's mind, the images near Gilgal would be symbols of foreign domination.

Abominations from Moab

For the reader of Judges who is familiar with the rest of the Hebrew Scriptures, Moab in this narrative will evoke thoughts of Moab, the source of "abominations" in Israel in later years. Solomon took a Moabite princess as one of his queens (1 Kgs. 11:1) and built a shrine for Chemosh outside Jerusalem (v. 7). He did the same for his Ammonite queen, whose god bore the title of Milcom, "king" (1 Kgs. 11:5). Since Chemosh is also called god of the Ammonites (Judg. 11:24), it is likely that both Chemosh and Milcom were variant names of the same star-god, Ashtar. (Cf. the name "Ashtar-Chemosh," Moabite Stone, line 17; Williams, "Moabite Stone," *IDB* 3:420.) John Gray ("Molech, Moloch," *IDB* 3:422-23) believes that Molech, with the same first three consonants as Milcom, is not the name of another god, but another spelling of the same title, meaning "king." It is of interest to note that these three names or titles—Chemosh, Milcom, and Molech—are singled out by the writer of 1 Kgs. 11:5, 7 to carry the epithet "abomination."

The term "abomination" (which is the RSV translation for two different Hebrew words) is associated with the practice of human sacrifice (cf. Jer. 7:30-31) and ritual sexual coupling (Jer. 13:27). According to George E. Mendenhall (*The Tenth Generation* [Baltimore: Johns Hopkins University Press, 1973], 111), the practice of ritual intercourse and ritual murder may have originated in Moab and Gilead. The Moabite king Mesha sacrificed his oldest son to Chemosh (2 Kgs. 3:27), and Ahaz followed suit (2 Kgs. 16:3). The custom of human sacrifice was associated with the worship of Molech (Lev. 18:21; 20:2-5). It was widespread in the northern kingdom of Israel (2 Kgs. 17:17), as well as in Judah down to the days of Josiah (2 Kgs. 23:10).

One of the abominations was incest, attested in the laws of Leviticus (Lev. 18:6-18; 20:10-21). The strange tradition that Moab and Ammon were the offspring of an incestuous union of Lot with his two daughters may preserve an aversion for Moabite and Ammonite sexual immorality (see below, p. 76, "Perspectives," no. 2).

GOD'S DELIVERER

An Unlikely Choice

Aside from Othniel, the model judge from Judah, the heroes of the book of Judges are unlikely candidates for the title "deliverer"

(Judg. 3:15). Ehud, for example, was no warrior. His right hand was useless, possibly deformed or maimed (the literal meaning of the Hebrew term translated "left-handed" is "handicapped in the right hand"). The seven hundred skilled slingers of Benjamin (20:16) were probably more like what we mean by "left-handed," or possibly ambidextrous (1 Chron. 12:2). Ehud's name is a variant spelling of the Hebrew word *ehad,* meaning "one." The name could thus mean "loner" (Boling, *Judges,* 85). Yet God chose this handicapped loner and "raised" him up as *the* Benjaminite (Judg. 3:15) who would liberate his people (see below, p. 76, "Perspectives," no. 3).

God's Initiative

Ehud was not a self-made man. God's initiative in Ehud's life was similar to his action in breaking "the bars of your yoke" in Egypt through his servant Moses, and making his people "walk erect" (Lev. 26:13). The story of Ehud is one more example of Israel's faith that God is always ready to "raise up" "all who are bowed down" (Ps. 145:14), including "the poor . . . [and] the needy," from the "dust" of a deathlike existence and the "ash heap" of degradation (1 Sam. 2:8). Ehud was God's "horn of salvation" (Luke 1:69; cf. Ps. 148:14), "raised up" by God to liberate his people so that they could again walk erect in freedom and dignity.

A Mysterious Process

The expression "raised up" implies a purposeful process which led to the dramatic events of this narrative. We first meet Ehud working alone, perhaps in secret, on his assassination weapon (Judg. 3:16). He had been appointed leader of the tribute delegation. We are left to imagine what events or influences lay behind his daring decision to put an end to the oppression.

Had he been "radicalized" by personal participation in the humiliating annual tribute ceremony in previous years? This would help explain his apparent familiarity with ceremonial protocol (3:17) as well as the architectural details of the Moabite audience chamber (vv. 20, 23). Had he been under the influence of the levitical priests, the "teachers, theologians, storytellers, counsellors, and inspired preachers of the new society" (E. John Hamlin, *Inheriting the Land,* 145), the "primary bearers of Yahwism in premonarchic times" (Norman K. Gottwald, *The Tribes of Yahweh,* 320)? This would explain Ehud's bold resolve to rid his people of foreign domination and his confidence that Yahweh would give him victory (v. 28).

Was he associated with the seers of early Israel who had the task of "championing the inheritance of the Mosaic period, and of maintaining in the face of foreign influences the character which the worship of God had acquired as a result of Moses' work" (Walther Eichrodt, *Theology of the Old Testament.* Old Testament Library [Philadelphia: Westminster and London: SCM, 1961], 1:297-98)? If Ehud had a reputation as a seer, this could explain why Eglon welcomed Ehud as the apparent bearer of a divine oracle after he had been at "the sculptured stones near Gilgal" (3:19, 26). A former king of Moab had welcomed Balaam the seer in similar fashion (Num. 22:36).

LIBERATION

With Eglon having made his annual trip across the Jordan from the east bank to receive tribute from his Israelite vassals, we are ready for the rapid movement of the story. Let us follow the movement and the deeper levels of meaning by looking at key words which the storyteller repeats for special emphasis and meaning.

As the story begins, the people of Israel are in Eglon's power (Judg. 3:13-14; cf. 2:14; RSV "power" translates the Hebrew word *yad,* which means "hand"). Ehud's handicapped *right hand* (3:15) was the asset that gave him access to the king's inner chamber. The people of Benjamin sent their tribute of grain, fruit, oil, and animals by Ehud's (left) *hand* (RSV "by him," v. 15). It was indeed his *left hand* which struck the unexpected blow against the oppressor (v. 21) and freed Israel from his "hand" (cf. 8:22).

We note the ironic use of the word "fat," first to describe the king's life of luxury at the expense of the humiliating impoverishment of his vassals (3:17). In the next moment his corpulence becomes the place of extreme vulnerability to the death blow (v. 21), as the fat closes over the dagger (v. 22). Luxury turns into degradation as the "rich fool" (cf. Luke 12:16-20) lies fallen in his own excrement (Judg. 3:22). Likewise, the "cool roof chamber," a place of private relaxation and pleasure for the king following the lengthy presentation ceremony (vv. 20, 24), becomes his death chamber, a place of blood and filth (vv. 23, 25).

Two "messages" (Heb. *dabar,* "word/act") appear at the center of the story. The first message is "secret" (v. 19). The king understands this to mean a word to be given in private by what he supposes to be a harmless Hebrew seer. The word translated as "secret" can also mean "covering" (cf. 1 Sam. 25:20). Ironically, the king's own flesh becomes the covering for the "message," which takes the form of a dagger (see below, p. 77, "Perspectives," no. 4).

The second message is "from God" (Judg. 3:20). The king takes this to mean an oracle from the divine world, perhaps by way of astrology (cf. Isa. 47:13), or omens (cf. Num. 24:1), or hepatoscopy (looking at a sheep's liver; cf. Ezek. 21:21). The Israelite reader knows that this "word/act" is from the Maker of heaven and earth (Ps. 121:2) and the LORD of all nations (Ps. 86:9). Like the mysterious message on the wall (Dan. 5:24-28), this meant the end of Moabite power in Israel.

Finally, the "sculptured stones" (or, more likely, the "graven images") frame the action of the story. Ehud "turned back" at that point to begin his fateful mission (Judg. 3:19). The Hebrew text states that he turned "from" the images. The surface meaning is simply that at this point he turned around. At a deeper level, Ehud is seen as a true Israelite who turns from the seductive influence and enslaving power of Molech/Milcom/Chemosh in order to end the domination of Molech in Yahweh's land. Finally, Ehud "passed beyond" the images (v. 26). The deeper meaning is that he has crossed over beyond their influence and power to organize the resistance and once again create space for the new society envisaged in Josh. 13–22 (cf. Hamlin, *Inheriting the Land,* 109-73).

PERSPECTIVES

1. *The Ways of a King (see above, p. 71)*

The Eglon-Chemosh model may have been one inspiration for Samuel's warning about "the ways of the king" (1 Sam. 8:10-17).

According to this model the image of Chemosh in Jerusalem (1 Kgs. 11:7) would have influenced Solomon in putting the "heavy yoke" (1 Kgs. 12:4) on the northern tribes which led to their revolt (v. 16). This should prompt us to look for the Eglon-Chemosh model of oppression in our world today. Some would find it in small dictators like Somoza or Idi Amin, while others would see it in the pattern of domination by the superpowers.

2. Moab in God's Plan (see above, p. 72)

Eglon as an imperial overlord was first a *tool* employed by God (Judg. 3:12) and then an *obstacle* to God's plan for Israel. Ehud removed the obstacle (3:30). However, Moab as a cultural, historical, and national entity was *a part of God's plan* for "all the peoples" of the world (Ps. 67:3). God's servant people as "a light to the nations" (Isa. 49:6; cf. Gen. 12:3) would have a part in the restoration of Moab "in the latter days" (Jer. 48:47).

3. Benjamin in Context (see above, p. 73)

The tribe of Benjamin should be seen as one part representing the whole "people of Israel." In each of the dramatic episodes the Scribe focuses attention on different representative segments of the whole people. In this case the sin, punishment, cry of distress, and liberation of "the people of Israel" (Judg. 3:12, 14, 15) involved the tribe of Benjamin in particular.

In order to see this incident in the Scribe's perspective, we should look *back* to the reference to Benjamin in the prologue (1:21; see above, pp. 28-29) and *forward* to the story of Benjamin in the epilogue (chs. 19–21). In this perspective, the new round of evil deeds begun by Benjamin (3:12) appears to be the "Canaanite way of death" (see above, pp. 15-16) learned from the Jebusites in Jerusalem, the "city of foreigners" (19:12). At the same time, the brutal crime of the Benjaminites of Gibeah (19:25) and the bitter civil war against Benjamin (ch. 20) seem to reveal the temporary character of the liberation won by Ehud.

4. *The Sword of the Spirit (see above, p. 75)*

The picture of Ehud at work on his sword (3:16) leads our thoughts to "the sword of the Spirit, which is the word of God" (Eph. 6:17), with which the Christian struggles against the Eglon-Chemosh type of "principalities, . . . powers, . . . world rulers . . . [and] spiritual hosts of wickedness" (v. 12). Ehud's "message" was a political act (sword). Does the term "sword of the Spirit" rule out the possibility of political action? Does "the word of God . . . living and active, sharper than any two-edged sword" (Heb. 4:12) apply to nations as well as to individuals? We could think of Ehud's sword as piercing the inner being of Moab to cut out the imperial ambitions for expansion. The NT "Savior" (Acts 13:23; the Hebrew word translated "deliverer" in Judg. 3:9, 15 may also be translated "savior," as in the NAB) speaks words like "a sharp two-edged sword" (Rev. 1:16; 2:12) with which he wars against idolaters (2:16) and "smites" the nations (19:15; cf. Judg. 1:25). Using the Ehud model, these "sharp" words have clear political implications.

SHAMGAR,
THE FOREIGN DELIVERER
Judges 3:31

THE FIRST PHILISTINE OPPRESSION

The appearance of the Philistines in the Shamgar incident is generally believed to be an anachronism, because the Philistines came later, in the time of Samson (Judg. 13:1). Was the Scribe using historical tradition here? From historians we learn that some "Sea Peoples" from the Mediterranean islands had invaded the Syrian coast in the late 13th century. By the time of Ehud they were moving down into the coastal areas of Palestine. Since the Philistines who arrived on the scene later were also "Sea Peoples," we might term these invaders as "pre-Philistine" (Robert G. Boling, *Judges*, 90; see above, pp. 34-35, 49). After Ehud's death, these "pre-Philistines" were pressing in on the Israelite tribes "in the days of Shamgar, son of Anath" (5:6; William F. Albright, *Yahweh and the Gods of Canaan*, 49).

Since Shamgar is associated with Ehud, who won a victory on the east near Jericho, it is possible that this victory frustrated a thrust from the west along the road up from Gezer (1:29) and on to Gibeon, Bethel, Jericho, and the "King's Highway" in Transjordan (see above, p. 44).

GOD'S DELIVERER

The Strange Savior

The strangeness of the heroes in Judges continues with Shamgar. He was of Hurrian descent and had been a worshipper of a Canaanite goddess. But the important fact was that he, like Ehud, "delivered" Israel. His name means "a gift from Shimike," who was god of the Hurrians. The Hurrians had been powerful in north-western Mesopotamia centuries earlier, but some of them lived in Palestine in the time of the judges. They are known in the Bible as Horites, and perhaps Hivites. The name itself shows that Shamgar's family was not Israelite (the equivalent name in Hebrew would be Jonathan, "gift from Yahweh").

The other part of his name is "son of Anath." Anath was a popular Canaanite goddess whose name was preserved in the place name Beth-anath (1:33; see above, p. 46). We may tentatively assume that Shamgar had been a worshipper of Anath. It may be that his military bravado was inspired by this goddess of battles who, according to myth, rejoiced ecstatically over the slaughter of her human enemies (Albright, 124). Shamgar may have been an adopted Israelite.

LIBERATION

The Scribe has arranged the story of Ehud in such a way as to place Shamgar *after* (i.e., toward the end of) Ehud's long peace (3:30) but *before* Ehud's death (4:1). Shamgar thus appears in this brief section not as a judge in his own right, but as one who helped preserve Ehud's long peace by a single-handed victory over a party of six hundred armed men pushing up along the road from the coast. Perhaps the Scribe saw this as a partial fulfillment of Joshua's word that "one man of you puts to flight a thousand" (Josh. 23:10; cf. Judg. 15:15 for Samson's complete fulfillment). If so, he must have believed that God was using Shamgar to fight for Israel (Josh. 23:15; see below, "Perspectives").

PERSPECTIVES

Shamgar in Context

The grisly scene in which the hero slaughters six hundred armed men with a primitive agricultural weapon seems more like a dance in a folk drama about a legendary hero than an actual eyewitness account. Shamgar's single-handed victory may be alluded to in a later reference to the LORD's deliverance of Israel "from the Philistines" (Judg. 10:11). Shamgar is like David's "mighty men"

Eleazar and Shammah, who also fought single-handedly against the Philistines, inflicting even heavier casualties than Shamgar (2 Sam. 23:9-12). Shamgar thus points the reader forward to David, who finally subdued the Philistines (2 Sam. 8:1), and to Jesus Christ, who was God's deliverer to disarm "the principalities and powers," God "triumphing over them in him" (Col. 2:15). In the book of Judges, the victory is never complete. Shamgar's victory is but one incident in the increasingly bitter struggle against the powers of oppression and death.

DEBORAH,
THE WOMAN JUDGE

Judges 4:1–5:31

In these two chapters the Scribe has combined older prose and poetic materials into an intentional theological unity. As with the other stories of the judges, this one is an epic tale of sin (4:1), disciplinary suffering (v. 2; see above, p. 61) and cruel oppression (v. 3), followed by deliverance (vv. 23-24) and a generation of peace and justice (5:31b). A 12th cent. B.C.E. battle for control of the roads in the Esdraelon Valley of Galilee becomes a paradigm of God's support for his "friends" in opposition to his "enemies," the oppressors (5:31a; see below, pp. 86-87, "Perspectives," no. 1).

POLITICAL-MILITARY OPPRESSION

The Engine of Oppression

As king (4:2, 23, 24) of "the kings of Canaan" (5:19), Jabin is the Scribe's northern counterpart to Adoni-bezek in the south (1:5-7), symbol of Canaanite political power in the north. As commander of the fearsome corps of nine hundred iron chariots (4:3, 13) as well as a large fighting force, Sisera symbolizes the power of military technology in the service of oppressive political policy. This symbol would be well understood in the days of Jeremiah and the Scribe (Jer. 4:13; 6:23). In this account, military victory (Judg. 4:15-16) is the necessary first step toward ending political oppression (vv. 23-24).

Economic Strangulation

The meaning of the "cruel oppression" (4:3) is suggested in the poetic version of the battle. There we read of abandoned roads (5:6

81

NIV), with travel possible only by crooked back roads, and a pall of fear on village life (v. 7 NIV). This seems to point to the economic strangulation of the life of the Israelite villagers by control of the major trade routes, such as the west-to-east road from Dor to Beth-shean and the south-to-north road from Joppa to Hazor by way of Megiddo (see above, p. 44; see also Baruch Halpern, *The Emergence of Israel in Canaan,* 212-13, for the importance of control of trade routes in Judges). This interpretation of 5:6-7 is confirmed by the reference in v. 10 to roads once more open, following the Israelite victory over Sisera.

Plunder

We also learn that the kings of Canaan had been extracting unjust gain or "plunder" (5:19 NIV; cf. 2:14, 16) from the villagers. The term translated "spoils" (RSV) means, more specifically, "gain" made by violence, as in the case of Samuel's sons (1 Sam. 8:3) or, in the Scribe's time, Jehoiakim's "dishonest gain" (Jer. 22:17) and the "evil gain" of the rich people of Jerusalem (Hab. 2:9). The victory won by Barak meant that the kings of Canaan were no longer able to exploit the Israelite villagers in this way.

Rape

One final clue about oppression may be seen in the thoughts attributed to Sisera's mother, that her son might be dividing captive Israelite girls among the soldiers (Judg. 5:30). With Israelite poverty created by economic exploitation, and brute force in the hands of soldiers on raids, sexual violation of women would be common. This is one meaning of "afflict" (2:18). The Hebrew word may mean "to humble or force a woman sexually," as in 19:24, where it is translated "ravish" (see below, p. 165). Jael's cold-blooded murder of Sisera (5:26), Deborah's exultation over his death (v. 24), as well as the mocking tone in the portrayal of Sisera's mother (vv. 28-30) lead us to surmise that this general was particularly hated by women.

The period of oppression lasted "twenty years" (4:3), which is the Scribe's way of saying that this was the most serious threat to the unity and survival of the people thus far.

Note on Judges 5:7

Some scholars give a different interpretation of the phrase "the peasantry ceased," preferring to translate the verb as "grew fat," that is, on raids on Canaanite caravans (cf. Robert G. Boling, *Judges,* 109). The problem with this interpretation is that it does not fit with the climax of vv. 6-8, "until you arose . . . ," or the reference to the poor preparation of the militia for battle (v. 8). Another interpretation of v. 7 could be given which accepts the proposed translation along the lines suggested by Deut. 32:15-16, that "grew fat" refers to the capitulation of some of the oppressed people when they "forsook God."

GOD'S DELIVERER

A Mother in Israel (5:7)

The sudden appearance of Deborah, "a woman, a prophet" (Judg. 4:4, literal translation), is completely unexpected in "a collection of writings by males from a society dominated by males . . . portraying a man's world" (Phyllis A. Bird, "Images of Women in the Old Testament," 41-48). She is identified not by father, husband (RSV "the wife of Lappidoth" in 4:4 may well mean "spirited woman," according to J. Cheryl Exum ["Deborah," in *Harper's Bible Dictionary,* 214]), or son, but rather as "a mother in Israel" (5:7).

Compassion for her divided and oppressed "children" made Deborah act to redress their wrongs. Her vision of an alternative to her "children's" helplessness gave them strength to unite in a struggle for a transformed society. Her sense of timing, her faith in God, and her skill in strategic planning led to the end of Canaanite power in the north (4:23-24). Her wise warning to Barak to give up hope of personal glory on the road to war (v. 9) stands in sharp contrast to the words of the "wisest ladies" of Sisera's mother (5:29-30). Deborah's wise leadership gave her people a generation of stability (5:31b).

LIBERATION

Ferment in Ephraim

The ferment for reform that led to liberation began in the Ephraimite hill country under Deborah's palm tree (4:5), where the oppressed people came to her for relief from injustice. Canaanite economic oppression backed up by military power had begun to move down into Ephraim. According to the Scribe's time frame, this area had recently been liberated from Moabite colonial oppression on the east by Ehud (3:30) and from expansionist pressure from the pre-Philistine Sea Peoples on the west along the Gezer-Aijalon road by Shamgar (3:31). Deborah "arose" (5:7) "at that time" (4:4) as Israel's mother-savior.

The Galilee Flashpoint

The action takes place in Galilee (4:10), where, as the prologue has informed us (1:30, 33), Israelites and Canaanites lived together without obvious conflict. We may guess that this uneasy peace was broken by two factors. First was a growing dependence of the Israelite villagers on trade with the Canaanite cities (cf. 3:5-6). This would result in increasing exploitation by the cities and vulnerability to Canaanite practices and values, as suggested by the comment about "new gods" (5:8; cf. Deut. 32:17). Second, the peace was broken by the powerful coalition of Canaanite city-states (such as the four mentioned in Judg. 1:30, 33, and the seven in v. 31, called the "kings of Canaan" in 5:19). This Canaanite coalition was allied with the northern branch of the pre-Philistine Sea Peoples under Sisera (4:2).

War in the Gates (5:8)

From Deborah's Palm to Mt. Tabor. Deborah, inspired by Yahweh, made the decision for war, against the better judgment of Barak (4:8). This decision was made in response to the cries which the people brought to God (v. 3) through her (v. 5) as a prophet (v. 4). The nine occurrences of the Hebrew verb *halak* (here only in ch. 4) demonstrate the decision "go!" (v. 6), the debate "if you will go with me, I will go" (v. 8), and the rapid movement of Deborah and Barak to the north (v. 9) from Ephraim to Mt. Tabor. On their way north (v. 9), Deborah would be able to meet with the elders of the villages of Ephraim and Manasseh "in the gates" (5:8) to urge their participation in the liberation struggle (see below, p. 88, "Perspectives," no. 4).

Besides being a mountain sacred to the three northern tribes of Zebulun, Naphtali, and Issachar, Mt. Tabor was a military vantage point from which a militia of volunteers could challenge those in control of both the trade routes mentioned above. That is the reason Barak's muster on Tabor caused Sisera to field his chariot corps and troops (4:13).

From Tabor to Victory. In the poetic version we find five critical moments, indicated by the Hebrew word translated "then," describing the swift course of the battle. The sudden decision for war (5:8) is followed by the rush down the slopes of Tabor (vv. 11, 13), the counterattack of the "kings of Canaan" (v. 19), and the panic-stricken retreat of the chariot corps, bogged down in the muddy valley of the swollen Kishon River (vv. 21-22). For the ethical problem posed by Jael's murder of Sisera (4:21; 5:24-27), and the significance of Sisera's mother (5:28-30), see below, pp. 87-88, "Perspectives," nos. 2 and 3.

Note on the Tribal Participation in the Battle of Kishon

The mention of ten tribes implies a northern federation at this time. Only two tribes are mentioned in the prose narrative (4:6, 10), but four others appear in the poem as participants in the battle (5:14-15). Issachar (v. 15) joined Naphtali and Zebulun, since their territories join at Mt. Tabor. Perhaps we may assume that the three others (Benjamin, Ephraim, and Manasseh-Machir) were guarding the escape routes on the southern rim of the valley. This might account for the discrepancy between the ten thousand troops of the prose account (4:6, 10, 14) and the forty thousand of the poem (5:8). Some scholars suggest that the other four tribes (vv. 15-17) also participated in the battle. The list of tribes in Judg. 5 is interpreted as a "tribal muster" at a covenantal assembly recalling the victory. The absence of Judah is most noticeable and may mean that Judah was not yet fully a part of the tribal league.

Yahweh's Decisive Role

The reader learns that this war was planned by Yahweh, with victory promised in advance (4:6-7). Deborah encouraged Barak and his ten thousand militia with the words, "Does not the LORD go out before you?" (v. 14). Finally, Yahweh "struck terror into Sisera" (v. 15 JB; RSV "routed"). The same Hebrew verb appears in Joshua with the translation "threw them into a panic" (Josh. 10:10), in Exodus as "discomfited" (Exod. 14:24), and elsewhere as "throw . . . into great confusion" (Deut. 7:23; cf. Ps. 18:14; 144:6). In each case Yahweh is the subject, and the action involves natural phenomena (i.e., hail stones, the returning sea, or a lightning storm) to cause the panic among Israel's enemies.

As we read in the song, Yahweh caused the skies to pour down a torrential rain (Judg. 5:4), perhaps believed to be brought by the stars as servants of Yahweh (v. 20; cf. Ps. 103:21). This turned the Kishon River, usually a small stream with little water in the plain of Esdraelon, into an "onrushing torrent" that "swept them away" (Judg. 5:21) like "the torrents of perdition" (Ps. 18:4; cf. Isa. 30:28). It was this storm that threw Sisera and his chariot corps into a panic.

This intervention was proof that Yahweh, not Baal, controlled the forces of nature, in particular the storm that terrorized Sisera (cf. 1 Kgs. 17:1; 18:1, 45). It showed further that the stars were not "gods" but creatures and servants of Yahweh. Finally, Yahweh was the God of Sinai (Judg. 5:5), and his divine intervention was both to rescue his covenant partners from oppression and to give them "rest" (v. 31b) in order to create a new society of justice and freedom (cf. v. 23; see below, p. 89, "Perspectives," no. 5, for the idea of human "help" in the struggle).

PERSPECTIVES

1. Whose Point of View? (see above, p. 81)

Interpretation of this story in prose and poetry will depend on who is reading it and in what situation. Those who are suffering oppression will be able to identify the present-day equivalents of Jabin, the kings of Canaan, and Sisera. Those whose situation is not as difficult should try to read this narrative in solidarity with the oppressed. It could be that some readers would find themselves more like the oppressors than like the forces of Deborah and Barak! Those who would like to use the fervor or warlike emotions of this song in uncritical support of a nation or a cause would do well to examine the use of the word "perish" (5:31a) in Lev. 26:38 and Deut. 8:19-20.

2. *Jael in Context (5:24) (see above, p. 85)*

In the wider biblical context, the words "most blessed of women" are spoken only twice: by Deborah about Jael, and by Elizabeth about Mary (Luke 1:42). Yet the two women are completely different from each other. We must try to understand what lies behind these words in Jael's case.

In the first place, we should not look at Jael as a "model for morality," but rather as a "mirror for identity" (James A. Sanders, "Hermeneutics," *IDB*, Supplement, 406). The fact that Deborah called her "blessed" does not necessarily mean that God does the same. We should not be shocked at finding Jael's bloody deed recorded in the Bible, but rather we should look for similarities between ourselves and Jael.

Second, we should read Scripture in solidarity with the oppressed. If we put ourselves in the place of those who have suffered under tyrants like Hitler, Stalin, Somoza, or Idi Amin, we can understand how Deborah could call the woman who destroyed Sisera "blessed." As he had humiliated Hebrew women in the past, Sisera was now humiliated by a woman's hand. Deborah's words resonate with those of later prophets (Isa. 14:4b-7; Nah. 3:19).

Third, the "peace between Jabin the king of Hazor and the house of Heber the Kenite" (Judg. 4:17) was not an alliance which Jael betrayed by her act. Rather, it was an accommodation which the Canaanite political power made with the Kenite clan of itinerant smiths because of their valuable skills in metalworking. Indeed, the Canaanites may have been trying to gain control of this skill, since there was no "shield or spear" in Israel (5:8). The Kenites were converts to Yahwism from Mosaic days (4:11) and allies of Judah (1:16). Jael was acting in loyalty to Israel, as she understood her duty.

Finally, we may relate this act of Jael to Mary's words that God "has put down the mighty from their thrones, and exalted those of low degree" (Luke 1:52). Words spoken by Isaiah about God's plan to "break the Assyrian in my land" so that "his yoke shall depart from them" (Isa. 14:24-25) may help to put Sisera's defeat by Barak and his murder by Jael into the perspective of God's purpose for the whole earth (v. 26)—that through this people "all the families of the earth shall be blessed" (Gen. 12:3 RSV mg).

3. *The Haughty Queen (5:28-30) (see above, p. 85)*

We can get perspective on these verses by reading them alongside Isa. 47. Babylon is pictured there as a proud queen, a lover of pleasures, secure in her wickedness and opulence, who says in her heart, "I shall not sit as a widow or know the loss of children" (Isa. 47:8). Yahweh gave his people into her hands for disciplinary suffering, but Babylon overstepped the bounds set by the LORD of nations and showed God's people "no mercy" (Isa. 47:6). The words said of Babylon could be said of Sisera's mother: "evil shall come upon you, for which you cannot atone; . . . ruin shall come on you suddenly, of which you know nothing" (v. 11). We may also hear overtones of Amos' harsh words about the women of Samaria (Amos 4:1-3) or Isaiah's about the women of Jerusalem, with their luxurious living from the fruits of oppression (Isa. 3:16-24).

4. *Remembering Deborah (see above, p. 85)*

In keeping with her role as "a mother in Israel," Deborah modestly disappears from the narrative after her inspiring words to Barak on Mt. Tabor (Judg. 4:14). When later generations remembered this incident, they thought of Barak the man instead of Deborah the woman (1 Sam. 12:11; Heb. 11:32; cf. Ps. 83:9). However, Deborah lives on in the words of her song of justice and hope (Judg. 5), calling on later "Deborahs" to "awake, . . . utter a song" (v. 12) again. Christians have remembered her inspiring courage in the hymn "March on, O soul, with strength! . . . 'gainst lies and lusts and wrongs . . . (George T. Coster, from Judg. 5:21, *The Hymnal* [Philadelphia: Presbyterian Board of Christian Education, 1933], 273).

5. Helping God (see above, p. 86)

The only instance in the OT in which the word "help" (Heb. *'azar*) is used of humans helping God is in the curse on Meroz (Judg. 5:23; repeated for emphasis). Elsewhere we learn that God is deeply disappointed when no one answers his call (Jer. 7:13; Isa. 50:2; 59:16; 63:5) for "fellow workers" (1 Cor. 3:9). Abraham J. Heschel has said that "God needs . . . partners" who "aid God so that His justice and compassion prevail." Our supreme responsibility, says John Merkle, paraphrasing Heschel, is "to help liberate God from captivity and let the divine mercy flow through our lives to save the innocent who suffer" (John C. Merkle, "Abraham Joshua Heschel: The Pathos of God," *Christianity and Crisis* 45 [1985]: 495).

GIDEON, THE FLAWED JUDGE

Judges 6:1–9:57

A New Cycle

The Gideon-Abimelech story takes up one quarter of the book of Judges and is thus the most important single episode in the entire book. Jewish tradition groups Gideon, Jephthah, and Samson together as "the three least worthy of the judges" (Nahum M. Sarna, "Gideon," 558). Each of them is seriously flawed when compared with Othniel, Ehud, and Deborah. Thus begins the second sequence of deterioration according to the Scribe's view of the time of the judges (see above, pp. 59-60).

Beginning with Gideon we find for the first time the ambiguity of life in the Promised Land: intertribal tension (Judg. 8:1-3), savage and destructive local conflict (9:26-55), a fateful struggle for power involving a canaanized kingship (9:1-6), and a more defined focus on the political side of Baalism (8:33; 9:4, 46). Gideon is the last judge to give the land "rest" (8:28). His son Abimelech engulfed the land in violence and chaos, and no more "rest" is recorded in the book of Judges.

One Story: Gideon and Abimelech

In these four chapters the Scribe has combined a number of ancient narratives into a unity of his own design. This unity appears in patterns of words and ironic symmetries between the parts. Here are some examples:

Three Trees. The first tree marks Yahweh's purposive self-revelation (6:11, 19). The second is the site of Abimelech's unblessed coronation (9:6), while the third is the scene of Abimelech's ambush against his own people (v. 37).

90

Three Towers. When Gideon tore down the tower of Penuel and slew the men of the city (8:17), he little dreamed that his son would imitate him at the tower of Shechem. There Abimelech burned one thousand men and women to death (9:46-49), and he died trying to burn the tower of Thebez (vv. 51-54).

Six Flames of Fire. There is a stunning contrast between the flame of grace at the call of Gideon (6:21) and the flame of liberation from oppression in Gideon's three hundred torches (7:20), on the one hand, and the flame of anger and curse in the prophecy of Jotham (9:15, 20), the flame which made a holocaust of the citizens of Shechem (v. 49), and the flame intended for the people of Thebez (v. 52), on the other.

Ironic Symmetries. Included are the following: (1) The story begins with the wasting of the fertile land of Jezreel by the Midianites (6:5). At the end, Gideon's son Abimelech makes the land of Shechem a salty waste (9:45). (2) God comes to meet Gideon at his winepress (6:11), but the drunken revelers at the grape harvest festival plan revolt against Gideon's son (9:26-28). (3) The thorns and briers used by Gideon to punish the men of Succoth (8:7, 16) anticipate the harshness of Jotham's speech (9:14-15).

THE OPPRESSION: IMPOSED FAMINE

No Sustenance in Israel

Midianite oppression created a seven-year famine (6:1) among the tribes living around the valley of Jezreel (v. 33). This drove them into caves in the hills in order to escape the oppressors (v. 2) and brought them near to total disintegration, or, as the Scribe says, "very low" (v. 6). The camel-riding invaders were as numerous and destructive as locusts (v. 5; 7:12; cf. Joel 1:4; 2:3). They destroyed grain in the fields, plundered livestock (Judg. 6:4), and made the fertile fields into a wasteland (v. 5; see below, p. 103, "Perspectives," no. 1). Their power penetrated as far as Dor on the coastal road that led south to Gaza (v. 4). Scorched earth was their deliberate policy to break the power and will of the Israelites. They almost succeeded (see below, p. 103, "Perspectives," no. 2).

A Midianite Trading Empire

Norman K. Gottwald (*The Tribes of Yahweh*, 431-32, 463) has suggested a reason for Midianite policy. While continuing their pastoral-nomadic society, the Midianites were attempting to develop a trading empire along the "king's highway" which ran between Damascus and the Gulf of Aqabah through Ammon, Moab, and Edom. They needed to control those states and to have access to the east-west roads leading from the Mediterranean coast. One of the most important of these ran from Dor on the coast to Beth-shean at the eastern end of the valley of Jezreel. Control of this road would give them access and potential domination of the north-south trade route from Egypt to Mesopotamia. A subdued northern Israel would suit this purpose well.

GOD'S RELUCTANT DELIVERER

Preparing the Way: Covenant Teaching

Gideon, like Jesus, had a forerunner, a nameless "voice of one crying in the wilderness" (Mark 1:3). Like John the Baptist (John 1:6), this prophet, appearing at the beginning of the Gideon story, was on a special divine mission (Judg. 6:8) at that particular time. He was to tell the oppressed people in their caves and dens that the covenant LORD who brought them out of slavery was ready to save them again and make the wasteland fruitful, if they would only listen and obey. Covenant words of the past (Exod. 20:2) were spoken again: "I am the LORD your God"!

He told them the reason for their suffering: they had been drawn into the magnetic force-field of the "gods of the Amorites" and their way of death (see above, pp. 15-16). The first step in throwing off the yoke of "the people of the East" (oppressors; Judg. 6:3) was to break the hold of the gods of the Westerners (the literal meaning of "Amorites"; Robert G. Boling, *Judges,* 125, sees an intentional pairing of the words). Only when they chose Yahweh (Josh. 24:15) could they find freedom from oppression.

92

Beginning the Action: God's Faint-Hearted Man

Gideon was not handicapped like Ehud, or a foreigner like
Shamgar, or a person who was not expected to show leadership like
Deborah. His father owned the property on which the city shrine
was built (Judg. 6:25). He had servants at his disposal (v. 27). He
and his brothers had a kingly bearing (8:18). Gideon's trouble was
more psychological. He was overwhelmed by the disaster which
had come on his people and doubtful of God's power to deliver
(6:13). He suffered an inferiority complex because of the small size
of his clan and his own minor position in his family (v. 15). He
kept asking God for signs (vv. 17-18, 36-40) and was overcome by
fear that he had been too close to God, even though the initiative
lay with God (v. 22). Yet he was God's choice.

The Call

The narrative is a window into the ways of God with his chosen
one:

Surprise. "The LORD is with you" (6:12)! This greeting, with
its intensity of meaning for the individual at that particular
moment in time, is like Gabriel's greeting to Mary (Luke 1:28)
rather than a declaration of God's constant presence (as in Ps.
23:4).

Confidence-building. The words "mighty man of valor" (Judg.
6:12) show God's faith in what Gideon could become. Compare
them with Jesus' words to Peter in John 1:42.

Commission. "Go . . . deliver Israel" (Judg. 6:14)! Note how
the angel "turned to him," looking him straight in the eye.

Empowerment. "I will be with you" (v. 16)! Readers would
know that Gideon must have recognized the words spoken to
Moses (Exod. 3:12) and taken heart. Again we may compare them
with Jesus' farewell words (Matt. 28:20).

Confidence-building Again. "You shall smite the Midianites as
one man" (Judg. 6:16)! Gideon would be able to unite his own
scattered people to throw off the oppressor's yoke.

Divine Patience. "I will stay till you return" (v. 18).

Liturgical Instruction. "Take . . . put . . . pour" (v. 20).

Grace. "Peace be to you; do not fear, you shall not die" (v. 23).

93

Gideon's Response. God's blessing of *shalom* (peace) and Gideon's spontaneous construction of an altar to the God of *shalom* (Judg. 6:23-24; cf. Eph. 2:14) indicate that the new creation implied in the prophet's message was already beginning. *Shalom* carries the sense of power to live, protection against the forces of death and destruction, and divine favor in all undertakings (cf. Num. 6:24-26). *Shalom* is living space for a community of freedom, justice, and "disciplined holiness" (see above, pp. 60-61). *Shalom* is God's plan for the whole earth and all nations (Isa. 2:4; 9:7; 11:6-9; Luke 2:14). Gideon's altar in Ophrah, at what was formerly a Baal shrine beneath the oak tree, symbolizes Israel's vocation to bear witness to this new order of *shalom* in the world, "to the far and to the near" (Isa. 57:19; cf. Eph. 2:17; cf. Paul D. Hanson, "War and Peace in the Hebrew Bible," 347-48).

Confrontation

The fire which sprang up from the rock, perhaps at nightfall as with Abraham (Gen. 15:17), ignited a spark in Gideon's heart. The spark might have sputtered out after he had built the altar, if Yahweh had left him alone. The narrative makes it clear that Yahweh would not relax his pressure on his reluctant deliverer. The beginning of *shalom* meant an inevitable confrontation with the anti-*shalom* forces.

Breaking down the Baal altar and cutting down the wooden Asherah were commanded in Israelite law (Exod. 34:13; Deut. 7:5) and repeated in Covenant Teaching (Judg. 2:2). Yahweh's repetition of this command that same night in the case of Joash's altar and Gideon's fear of his own relatives and the men of Ophrah (6:27) suggest the degree of Baalism's fatal attraction for the people of Israel (see below, pp. 103-4, "Perspectives," no. 3).

When Gideon built the second altar at night he was secretly constructing a new world not of chaos but "to be inhabited" (Isa. 45:18), as we see in the expression "in due order" (Judg. 6:26; cf. 1 Kgs. 18:31). The altar was for the worship of the God of the covenant, "the LORD your God" (Judg. 6:26), echoing the prophet's words (v. 10). The wood for the sacrifice was the Asherah pole that had been cut down. A later prophet's satirical reflection strikes the same note: "Half of it he burns in the fire; over the half he eats flesh

. . . warms himself . . . And the rest of it he makes into a god, his idol" (Isa. 44:16-17; see below, p. 104, "Perspectives," no. 4).

Joash's defence of his son against the fearful and angry men of Ophrah suggests uncertainty about whether Yahweh and Baal were different names for the same God, or whether Yahweh was a male deity who might need a female consort. Was there a God of the covenant alongside the gods of nature and nation? In present-day terms it might be this: is there the God of the Church whom we worship on Sundays, alongside other gods of the marketplace, the nation, and the battlefield?

Joash took the pragmatic point of view: if Baal is God, he needs no one to save his reputation (RSV "defend his cause") against this subversive act (Judg. 6:31). In fact, Baal should prove his divine nature by saving the Israelites from the Midianites. As on Mt. Carmel, Baal was silent (1 Kgs. 18:26, 29).

The Spirit of Yahweh

The Midianites, correctly seeing Gideon's breaking down the altar of Baal and building an altar to the LORD as subversive, marshalled their forces to crush the rebellion (Judg. 6:33). Gideon seems to have hesitated again. This time God's intervention was not by an angel messenger, nor by a voice at night, but by a presence moving into Gideon's personal life in a special kind of incarnation (v. 34). The RSV translation "took possession" sounds like a violent invasion, as in the case of Samson (14:6) or Saul (1 Sam. 11:6). The Hebrew says something different: that God's Spirit put on Gideon's personality like a garment. [Note: This Hebrew idiom is used of only two other people in the OT: Amasai (1 Chron. 12:18; RSV "came upon") and the prophet Zechariah (2 Chron. 24:20; RSV "took possession of"). In neither case does it imply a sudden surge of strength.] Gideon is here like Joshua, "in whom is the spirit" (Num. 27:18) and who was "full of the spirit of wisdom" (Deut. 34:9). The indwelling Spirit of Yahweh brought not extraordinary physical power to Gideon, but wisdom to deliver his people by clever strategy (cf. Eccl. 9:15). When Gideon sounded the trumpet summoning his clan (Judg. 6:34), his tribe, and three other tribes (v. 35), it was Yahweh's Spirit directing him from within.

95

The Sign of the Fleece (6:34-40)

In spite of the personal presence of Yahweh's Spirit, Gideon still had his doubts. Like the people of Israel in the wilderness (Exod. 17:7; Ps. 95:9), he put the LORD to the test. Could Yahweh control the fall of dew?

Dew is a symbol of plenty given (Gen. 27:28) or withheld (v. 39), of security, prosperity, salvation, and victory—in short, of _shalom_ (Deut. 33:28-29). God's blessing on Israel is like the gentle descent of dew (Hos. 14:5-6). The test was this: Could Yahweh give or withhold this blessing? Or was it Baal who gave these things? Gideon received his answer and was ready to lead his people (see below, pp. 104-5, "Perspectives," no. 6).

LIBERATION ACCOMPLISHED

The Problem of Military Victory

Behind the story of the reduction of Gideon's fighting force (Judg. 7:2-7) was the risk God took in giving victory to his people. They would claim the credit for their own weapons and strategy: "My own hand has delivered me" (v. 2). This would be a self-glorification against God. This verse sends us back to 6:36, where Gideon seeks assurance that God will "deliver Israel by my hand." It also sends us forward to the request of "the men of Israel" that Gideon rule over them, "for you have delivered us out of the hand of Midian" (8:22), with no reference to the real Deliverer.

Gideon's Strange "Weapons"

The empty jars, the torches, and the trumpets which brought the astonishing victory may be seen as an "elaborate prank" which worked on the superstitions of the Midianites (Boling, _Judges,_ 147). At another level, we may look at their symbolic meaning, without discussing the question of the original intention of the narrator.

First, the _jars_. A jar is an earthenware vessel made by a potter, who may do as he likes with the vessel (Isa. 29:16; 45:9). God, the divine potter (Isa. 64:8), may declare "concerning a nation or a kingdom, that I will pluck up and break down and destroy it"

96

(Jer. 18:7). When Jeremiah broke the earthen flask, his act was a symbolic reference to Yahweh's decision to "break this people and this city, as one breaks a potter's vessel" (Jer. 19:11).

The jars in the hands of Gideon's three hundred were "empty" (Judg. 7:16; Heb. *reqim*). Surely the Scribe intends a pun here, using the same Hebrew word which describes Abimelech's "worthless" hirelings (9:4; cf. 11:3). The pun suggests that the jars were not only empty but worthless. Like the "kings of the earth" who set themselves "against the LORD" only to be broken in pieces "like a potter's vessel" (Ps. 2:2, 9), the Midianite oppressors had exceeded the boundaries set for them by God (Deut. 32:8) and would suffer the same fate. Gideon's men were performing a symbolic act similar to that of Jeremiah (Jer. 19:10-11).

The *torches* are best understood as symbols of "salvation as a burning torch" in the sight of the nations (Isa. 62:1-2; cf. 60:1-3). When the potter's worthless vessel (the nation which has turned from its appointed task to oppression) has been broken, then the light of God's salvation will shine forth for all to see.

The *trumpets* on the hill of Moreh are like the warning on the mountains to the "inhabitants of the world" (Isa. 18:3) that God is about to act in judgment against the oppressor. They also herald a new age like the Jubilee Year (Lev. 25:9) in which the rights of the poor, the slave, and the landless will be restored (see E. John Hamlin, *Inheriting the Land,* 50).

The Self-Inflicted Defeat

From the point of view of military narrative, this "battle" has what Robert G. Boling calls an air of "contrived unreality" (*Judges,* 147). It sounds a bit like the victory won by a choir of priests over the enemy (2 Chron. 20:21-22). The message must lie beneath the surface. Perhaps it is this: in the long run, oppression is self-defeating because it violates God's purpose of "righteousness, justice, and equity" (Prov. 1:3). The broken jars of the oppressive system, the torches of the new age, and the trumpets of warning and promise brought division, doubt, anger, and confusion among the invaders because self-interest and power were their only motivation. When these could not hold them together, they became their own worst enemies.

LIBERATION IN DOUBT

Who Is in Charge? (8:1-3)

Ephraim's violent complaint against Gideon is the first note of discord in the book of Judges. Their anger seems to be rooted in their dominant position in the tribal alliance. Even though they were not directly affected by the Midianite oppression, a sudden victory by a member of a small clan in Manasseh would seem to threaten Ephraim's hegemony.

Gideon's Headstrong Violence

Across the Jordan River, Gideon had such great confidence in God that he began to take things into his own hands. When the cities of Succoth and Penuel refused to give him provisions for the militia in hot pursuit of the Midianites, Gideon threatened them with vengeful words (Judg. 8:7, 9) and punished them with exaggerated cruelty. One who has read of the "Spirit of the LORD" in Isa. 11:2 is left to conclude that Yahweh's Spirit (Judg. 6:34) had left Gideon at this point.

Whether the inhabitants of these cities in Gilead were Israelites of the tribe of Gad or Canaanites in alliance with Israel, the punishment of torture and death (8:16-17) far exceeds the offense (on threshing them with thorns and briers, see Jacob M. Myers, "The Book of Judges," 747). In a wider perspective, it may be compared with Syria's crime: "They have threshed Gilead with threshing sledges of iron" (Amos 1:3; cf. 2 Kgs. 13:7). The fire which followed Gideon's "threshing" (Judg. 9:15, 20, 49, 52) anticipates God's judgment of Syria (Amos 1:4).

Gideon's Personal Revenge

Zebah and Zalmunna, the two kings of Midian whom Gideon pursued with single-minded zeal (Judg. 8:5, 12), have symbolic names with special meaning related to their fate. "Zebah" means "sacrifice," referring to Gideon's revenge murder of the two for the death of his brothers (vv. 19, 21). "Zalmunna" means "protection withheld," describing Gideon's use of the LORD'S name to kill rather than to protect (cf. Prov. 24:11). They are remembered in Ps. 83:11-12 as coveting Israel's land. This narrative places the emphasis elsewhere. With the Midianite power completely broken (Judg. 8:10), there was no political or military reason for the capture and execution of these two kings. The once faint-hearted Gideon appears here as a man driven by an inordinate passion for revenge. In the wider perspective of other parts of the Hebrew Scriptures, this was usurping the authority of the one who said "vengeance is mine" (Deut. 32:35; cf. Rom. 12:19).

Kingship: The Great Refusal

Despite his flaws and his kingly bearing even in the eyes of his enemies (Judg. 8:18), Gideon showed his greatness when he refused the invitation of "the men of Israel" to accept the hereditary office of ruler or king. His refusal is in dramatic contrast to his son's cynical plot to seize royal power in Shechem.

Gideon's statement that "the LORD will rule over you" (8:23) brings many questions to the mind of the reader. Does it recall God's commission to *deliver* rather than to *rule* (6:14)? Is it related to Gideon's first altar (v. 24) and the belief that true *shalom* is not a matter of imposed authority but of participation by the people at all levels? Does it recall the assurance of the dew-soaked fleece that Yahweh was the true Deliverer who worked through Gideon (vv. 37-38)? Was Gideon returning to his former modesty (v. 15) and saying "I am not the one for this position," as in the reply of the trees in Jotham's fable (9:9)? In a wider context, is the question related to the one to come from the tribe of Judah (see above, p. 35) who would say, "When one rules justly over men, ruling in the fear of God . . . [he is] like rain that makes grass to sprout from the earth" (2 Sam. 23:3-4)?

Or is it possible that Gideon sensed guile among the delegation? Were there Ephraimites, perhaps from Shechem, who would like to use Gideon to enhance their own power? Was this a scheming invitation stemming from the political Baalism that flared up after Gideon's death (Judg. 8:33; cf. 2 Kgs. 17:7-8)?

Back to Baalism

Another ironic note in this story so full of ironies is that the hero who began the process of liberation by breaking down the altar and idols of Baal worship (Judg. 6:27) ended by creating a "snare" which, after his death, would lead the people back to the seductions of Baal and Asherah and away from Yahweh! Significantly, we find in 8:27 and 33 the only specific illustrations in the book of Judges of the sad comment in the theological essay that Israel "played the harlot after other gods and bowed down to them" in the Promised Land (2:17).

It was a very natural process. Gideon had displaced the Baal priests in Ophrah at Yahweh's command (6:27). He had performed the duty of a priest himself by offering a sacrifice at the oak shrine with divine blessing (vv. 19-21). He had offered the sacrificial bull on the Yahweh altar (6:26). He had successfully inquired of the LORD before going into battle as a priest should do (vv. 36-37; cf. 1 Sam. 23:9-12). It was quite natural for him to recall those moments and wish to make them permanent by seeking a priestly role for himself after he had refused the offer of royal power.

The Ephod

For his "self-consecration as a priest" (Baruch Halpern, *The Emergence of Israel in Canaan,* 227), Gideon used captured gold ornaments and royal garments requisitioned from his men (Judg. 8:24-27). With these he made an ephod, which was probably an "elaborate priestly vestment" (Boling, *Judges,* 160; cf. 1 Sam. 14:3; Exod. 28:6-8), to make inquiry of the LORD, possibly by the use of Urim (cf. 1 Sam. 28:6; Exod. 28:30). Apparently he kept it on display in the shrine at Ophrah. It was very popular among the people from far and near because of Gideon's reputation as a hero and a man close to God.

The problem is that the ephod seduced Gideon, his family, and all the people, leading them away from the covenant and from Yahweh (Judg. 8:27). The deterioration continued, especially after Gideon's death, until the object of their infatuation was not the ephod but the Baals (v. 33). Instead of being led by the Spirit of

Yahweh which had guided and empowered Gideon (6:34), they now were controlled by something like the "spirit of harlotry" which led the people astray without their even knowing it (cf. Hos. 4:12).

LIBERATION BETRAYED (9:1-57)

Abimelech's disastrous three-year reign as a petty Canaan-style king in Shechem brings the story of Gideon to its tragic end. The good done by Gideon (Judg. 8:35) in rescuing his people from Midianite oppression (9:17) was forgotten by the people and betrayed by his son. The Scribe has shown how the corrupt monarchic social structure of Canaanite society with its injustice, immorality, and tyranny was cleansed from the south (see above, pp. 28, 30, 33) and destroyed in the north by Deborah and Barak. Now he shows the reader the appearance of the same kind of corrupt government at Shechem. On a broader canvas, this chapter tells about the political dimensions of the choice between good and evil in the Promised Land (Deut. 30:19).

An attentive reader can detect echoes of the early chapters of Genesis. Something like the tree of the knowledge of good and evil (Gen. 2:17) grows in the Promised Land, and death related to eating its fruit is a grim reality. Abimelech's covetous desire for royal power resembles the thoughts of Eve in the garden (Gen. 3:6). Abimelech speaks to his kinsmen with the deceptive and beguiling accents of the serpent (Gen. 3:4-5). His brothers' blood cries out from the ground like Abel's to curse the murderer (Gen. 4:10; cf. Judg. 9:24, 56). The spirit of division which hastened the destruction of Abimelech's kingdom (9:23) recalls the divine action to confuse and scatter the builders of the tower of Babel (Gen. 11:7-8).

In the Promised Land the equivalent of the bitter fruit is political Baalism. The cult of Baal-berith supplies the motive and immoral undergirding for Abimelech's rise (Judg. 8:33; Heb. *berit* means "covenant"; we might call this god "Baal of the counter-covenant"). The temple treasury provided financial backing for his violent seizure of power (9:4). The temple stronghold was the death trap of the hunted Shechemites seeking refuge from Abimelech's madness (v. 46). The temple area with its sacred oak

where the conspirators held their tragic/comic coronation ceremony of the murderer (v. 6) was ironically the location of Joshua's
covenant ceremony (Josh. 24:25-27). At the shrine of Baal of the
countercovenant, past warnings about rebelliousness (Deut.
31:27), the difficulty of following the LORD (Josh. 24:19), and
the problem of resisting the gods of the Amorites (Judg. 6:10) in
the Promised Land took on a political significance.

The theological key to this chapter is the speech by Gideon's
youngest son Jotham, a refugee from Abimelech's terror (9:7-20).
His platform was Gerizim, the mountain of Covenant Teaching
(v. 7; cf. Josh. 8:33), overlooking the site of the ceremony of the
countercovenant. Three points stand out:

1. Abimelech (the bramble in the parable) was the wrong
person for doing what a king should do. He could give neither
security (shade) to the ordinary citizen, nor protection (refuge)
to the victim of injustice. He was not chosen by Yahweh (cf.
1 Sam. 9:17; 13:14; 16:12-13). He knew nothing of the royal
task to "defend the cause of the poor of the people, give deliverance
to the needy, and crush the oppressor" (Ps. 72:4). Political Baalism
knew only raw power and self-interest as the standards for a king
(cf. 1 Kgs. 21:8-14). Such corruption eventually destroyed the
productive work of the olive and fig trees and the vine which chose
the bramble to be king.

2. The men of Shechem did not act "in good faith and honor"
(Judg. 9:15, 16, 19). These are covenant words spoken by Joshua
(Josh. 24:14) and later by Samuel in relationship to the people's
demand for a king (1 Sam. 12:24). The men of Shechem acted
out of clan pride (Judg. 9:3) and a complete disregard for what
God had done through Gideon to free them from oppression (vv.
16-18).

3. The result of the Shechemites' desertion of the covenant for
the countercovenant was the fire of mutual destruction (9:20):
treachery between allies (v. 24), ambush and counterambush (vv.
25, 34-35, 43), plots of revolt (vv. 26-29), slaughter (vv. 43-45,
49), and ruin (v. 45). We see here a mirror image of the self-in-
flicted defeat of the Midianites with "every man's sword against
his fellow" (7:22). The Hebrew word for "fight" *(laham),* previously used to describe only wars of defense against the foreign
aggressor, is used here for the first time in Judges for internal

warfare in Israel (9:38, 39, 45, 52; see below, p. 104, "Perspectives," no. 5, and p. 108, for a further mention of *laham*).

God is silent in the story of Abimelech, in contrast to his active intervention when he called Gideon. His only activity is to send a spirit of division or suspicion (v. 23) to make sure that the tyrant and his supporters do not establish themselves and the cries of the blood of the slain do not go unheeded (vv. 24, 56-57).

PERSPECTIVES

1. A Wasteland (see above, p. 91)

A consultation in Manila on the hazardous consequences and by-products of science and technology called attention to "the rapid destruction and depletion of natural resources to such an extent that there will be little lowland forest left in South East Asia in ten years." The report also called attention to "the poisoning of oceans, seas, rivers, the atmosphere, soil, and food resources by chemicals, heavy metals, and radiation" (D. Gosling, *Church and Society Newsletter* 4 [June 1986]). This might be a modern equivalent of the Midianites laying the land waste (Judg. 6:5).

2. Oppressed Cave Dwellers (see above, p. 91)

The Israelites who were forced to live in caves (Judg. 6:2) were the first of a succession who sought refuge in caves to escape oppression by the Philistines (1 Sam. 13:6), Queen Jezebel (1 Kgs. 18:4), and the Babylonians (Isa. 42:22). Living in caves would be the experience of people in the time of troubles known as the Day of the LORD (Isa. 2:19). The author of Hebrews called these people heroes of faith (Heb. 11:38). Comparable living conditions today could be the shanty towns on the edge of the great cities of Asia, the mountain refuges of peasant rebels against state police, or even forced labor camps.

3. Structural Idolatry (see above, p. 94)

Kosuke Koyama as a young Japanese, standing dazed among the ruins of a fire-bombed Tokyo, pondered "the mysterious destructive power of idolatry in history," especially the cult of emperor worship. Four decades later he reflected on "the demonic power of idolatry" in relation to technology, nuclear weapons, political systems, and power structures. "Baal persists in human history," and history is "the story of confrontation between Yahweh and Baal," he writes (*Mount Fuji and Mount Sinai,* 3, 38-39, 215). Structural idolatries may be resisted by people of faith like Gideon who recognize them for what they are. What Gideon did, however, was more like a revolution which overturned the structure completely.

4. A Modern Example of Idol Destruction (see above, pp. 94-95)

In 1847 Hung Hsiu-chuan, a Chinese recently converted to Christianity by the work of Protestant missionaries and aflame with zeal against idols, entered a temple with his fellow crusaders. They beat the idol, dug out its eyes, pulled off its beard, broke off its arms, and tore its dragon robe to shreds, as the villagers looked on with consternation and horror. Hung seems like a latter-day Gideon! But a contemporary Chinese Christian comments that Hung, following his missionary mentor, had attacked not only the idol but Chinese culture as well. He was later blinded by ambition for power and brought destruction and death to his people (Choan-Seng Song, *The Compassionate God,* 203-4, 207-9). How was Hung different from Gideon?

5. A Good Beginning Followed by a Bad Ending (see above, pp. 102-3)

Abimelech is similar to later kings who came to power in Israel with great violence (1 Kgs. 15:29; 2 Kgs. 9–10) and built a society "on a foundation of murder and injustice" (Mic. 3:10 TEV). His story is a warning that movements which begin with divine approval and bring true liberation (like Gideon's) may end up in cynicism, cruelty, and terrible destruction.

6. Symbolism of the Fleece (see above, p. 96)

Gideon's fleece has fascinated readers of many generations. Jews (see Sarna, 559) have seen it as a symbol of their people, chosen (wet) or rejected (dry). Christian tradition has seen it as a symbol of the Church or the Virgin Mary (Hans-Ruedi Weber, *Immanuel* [Geneva: World Council of Churches and Grand Rapids: Wm. B. Eerdmans, 1984], 30). Cyril of Jerusalem (315-385 C.E.) used it in his instruction to new Christians: "There is a birth from God before all ages, and a birth from a virgin at the fullness of time. There is a hidden coming like that of rain on fleece, and a coming before all eyes, still in the future" (Cyril of Jerusalem, *Catechetical Lecture* XV:1).

TOLA AND JAIR,
TWO WISE ADMINISTRATORS
Judges 10:1-5

Timely Grace after Terror

The Scribe introduces the story of Jephthah with brief notices about two judges who served a total of forty-five years, though not necessarily one after the other. The phrase "after Abimelech" (Judg. 10:1) is linked by Hebrew grammatical structure to the theological note at the end of the story of Abimelech (9:56-57). Chaos and death are there seen as God's judgment on the wickedness of Abimelech and the people of Shechem. This was a liberation, not from the oppression of external enemies, but from the terror of Abimelech's reign as a canaanized king in Shechem. Tola's home was Shamir, probably south of Shechem, and therefore related geographically to the aftermath of Abimelech's reign. In that situation, the "men of Israel," who had dispersed after the tyrant's death and gone to live with their families (v. 55), would need sustained Covenant Teaching and the discipline of covenant law. We may think of Tola going about from place to place in the area around Shamir, something like Samuel (1 Sam. 7:15-17). Yet despite his twenty-three years of work, the events described in Judg. 12:1-6 show that Tola was not able to lay the groundwork for a lasting peace.

Jair, from the eastern branch of the tribe of Manasseh (Num. 32:40-41), lived in Bashan (Deut. 3:14) in what Israelis today call the Golan Heights, to the north of Gilead where Jephthah was to serve as judge. This administrator was apparently a man of some means, as testified by his thirty sons mounted on royal steeds. His sons, each in charge of a city, would have helped him in the Covenant Teaching and administration of justice, thus keeping evil from breaking out in northern Transjordan for twenty-

106

two years. Perhaps both Tola and Jair were supported in this ministry of teaching and discipline by resident Levites, who may afterwards have come to live in the levitical cities of Shechem and Ashtaroth (or Golan; cf. Josh. 21:21, 27; see E. John Hamlin, *Inheriting the Land,* ch. 14).

JEPHTHAH,
THE OUTCAST JUDGE
Judges 10:6–12:7

The Scribe composed this dramatic and tragic story from older materials during the reign of Jehoiakim, who was "shedding innocent blood, and . . . practicing oppression and violence" (Jer. 22:17), while his people were burning "their sons and their daughters in the fire" (Jer. 7:31), believing that this was approved by Yahweh (Johannes Pedersen, *Israel, Its Life and Culture* I-II: 319-20). It is a skillfully wrought narrative about an outcast who becomes a savior, a victor who becomes a victim of his own intemperate vow, a war of liberation against oppressors on the east followed by a bitter civil war against a jealous fraternal tribe on the west. Warfare, past and present, dominates this story in a special way, as we can see from the fact that the Hebrew word translated "fight" or "make war" *(laham)* occurs fifteen times in these three chapters—more frequently than in the entire book up to this point (see above, pp. 102-3).

Jephthah as a hero of faith (Heb. 11:32) is a complex and ambiguous character who is nevertheless a servant of God's purpose of salvation. We may indeed see ourselves and our times mirrored in this disturbing episode in the book of Judges.

THE OPPRESSION: LAND-GRABBING

Both the Gideon and the Jephthah stories are about land. In the first, a fertile land is laid waste by powerful outside commercial interests and an internal civil conflict. The Jephthah story is about conflicting claims of—and armed struggle for—possession and control of the land, involving social, economic, religious, and political issues.

108

The Economics of Land-Grabbing

Ammon's traditional territory was situated about 30 km. (20 mi.) east of the Jordan River, between the Jabbok River on the north and a line a few kilometers north of the Dead Sea on the south. The capital city of Rabbath-ammon (present day Amman, capital of Jordan) was strategically located at the point where the east and west branches of the King's Highway, the only trade and communication route between Elath and Damascus, converged (Yohanan Aharoni and Michael Avi-Yonah, *The Macmillan Bible Atlas*, map 78; Aharoni, *The Land of the Bible*, pp. 54-55 and map 3, p. 44). Along this road medicinal balm from Gilead (Gen. 37:25; 43:11; Ezek. 27:17; Jer. 8:22) as well as products from Egypt, Arabia, Canaan, Syria, and Mesopotamia would travel.

Ammon's economic advantage at Rabbath-ammon was limited by Israelite possession of land between Ammon and the Jordan River in the district of Gilead. Ammon's alliance with the Philistines, suggested in Judg. 10:7, may well have been due to converging trade interests (Norman K. Gottwald, *The Tribes of Yahweh*, 762 n. 340). Ammon, in control of the major trade route east of the Jordan, could gain by linking up with Philistia, which controlled the coastal road called in Roman days the Via Maris. The raids mentioned in v. 9 may be seen as Ammonite probes across Gilead, weakened by a defeat in "that year" (v. 8), to gain access to three roads from Jericho to the west: (1) the road in Judah leading to Kiriath-jearim, Beth-shemesh, and the coast, (2) the road in Benjamin leading to Gibeon, Beth-horon, and Gezer, and (3) the road in Ephraim leading to Bethel and Aphek.

Previously Ehud had blocked the Moabite/Ammonite attempt to get access to these roads, and Shamgar had stopped the "pre-Philistine" advance along the Gezer–Beth-horon road. Similar attempts in the north had been prevented by Deborah/Barak and Gideon. By Jephthah's time, there are hints from archaeology that the Philistines had extended their influence south from Bethshean to Succoth in the Jordan Valley, which had been alienated from Israel by Gideon's harsh punishment (8:16). Succoth was located just north of the Gileadite shrine city of Mizpah (G. Ernest Wright, "Fresh Evidence for the Philistine Story," 70-86).

In view of these unsuccessful attempts to link up with the Philistines on the coast, the Ammonite king's main concern was to consolidate his control of the King's Highway, since part of it ran through Israelite Gilead both south and north of Rabbath-ammon. To achieve this it would be necessary to expand to the west and take over land occupied by Israelites who lived in Gilead. The resulting eighteen-year occupation (10:8) forms the backdrop for the conflict in Jephthah's time.

The Theology of Land Loss

Where Sin Increased: Seven Harlotries (10:6-8). The Scribe uses familiar expressions, such as "again did what was evil," in order to place the Ammonite aggression in the framework of Yahweh's constructive anger (3:7-8, 12; 4:1-2; 6:1; see above, p. 61). But his enumeration of the gods of seven (10:6) of "the peoples who were round about them" (2:12) suggests an intention to portray this as the most extreme case of behavior "worse than their fathers" (2:19; see below, p. 123, "Perspectives," no. 1). In the words of the psalmist, the people of Israel mingled with the nations, learned their ways, and polluted the land (Ps. 106:35, 38), and thus lost control of it. The Scribe's reference to Israel's illicit love affair with the gods of seven peoples serves to prepare the reader not only for the grim events in the rest of the book of Judges, but also for the violent actions of later kings like Ahab, Manasseh, and Jehoiakim.

Readers in the time of the Scribe would recall that gods of three of the five nations (i.e., of Moab, Ammon, and Sidon; Judg. 10:6) were the chief sources of corruption in the court of King Solomon (1 Kgs. 11:1). Solomon showed his subservience to them by building a state system "upon coercion in which free citizens were enslaved for state goals" (Walter Brueggemann, *The Land,* 710). The gods of Sidon were identified with the evil influence of Queen Jezebel (1 Kgs. 16:31) on King Ahab (1 Kgs. 21:25-26), notorious for the royal confiscation of the land of Naboth (v. 16). All five of the nations in Judg. 10:6 appear in Amos' list of the aggressor nations who revealed their true nature by violating "the covenant of brotherhood" (Amos 1:9) with shocking violence, aggressive territorial expansion, brutal slave trade for economic gain and political domination (Amos 1:3, Syria; v. 6, Philistia; v. 9, Phoenicia; v. 13, Ammon; 2:1, Moab).

To serve the gods of these nations would mean to accept their values as norms for behavior (see below, p. 123, "Perspectives," no. 2). We have only to read passages about land-grabbing and oppression in Mic. 2:2; 3:1-3; Isa. 5:8 to understand how the values held by these nations could be internalized by the rich and powerful in Israel. Serving the gods of the oppressors could mean surrender of Israelite political and religious independence and conscription of Israelite manpower into their armies. Israelites would have to serve on feudally organized agricultural estates and tend flocks and herds. Serving foreign gods would cause the weakening or disappearance of Israelite social institutions and the impoverishment of the Israelite people (cf. Gottwald, *The Tribes of Yahweh*, 416-17). Furthermore, it would mean the corruption of those with property (such as Jephthah's father) in order to seek favor with the oppressors. This is the meaning of the word "oppressed" (Judg. 10:8), which translates a rare Hebrew word, recalling the consequences of covenant violation, that "you shall be only oppressed and crushed continually" (Deut. 28:33).

Grace Abounded: Seven Deliverances (10:11-16). In this third and final message from Yahweh to Israel (cf. Heb. 1:1), the Scribe presents seven acts of salvation to balance Israel's seven "harlotries" (Judg. 2:17; 8:33). In the first message, God had asked, "What is this you have done" (2:2)? In the second, he chided them: "You have not given heed to my voice" (6:10). Finally, God exclaims in exasperation, "I will deliver you no more" (10:13), and tells them to go to the other gods they have chosen for deliverance (v. 14; cf. Jer. 2:28).

Once Again, Repentance. On previous occasions Israel had simply cried for help, appealing to Yahweh's covenant obligation (Judg. 3:9, 15; 4:3; 6:7). At this solemn assembly, possibly at Mizpah of Gilead (cf. 11:11), for the first time in the book of Judges Israel shows a consciousness of corporate guilt. When God shows skepticism about the sincerity of the first confession, "we have sinned" (10:10; cf. Hos. 6:4), the people of Israel show signs of true repentance in three stages: (1) they repeat their confession; (2) they throw themselves on God's grace ("do to us whatever seems good to thee," Judg. 10:15); and (3) they take practical steps to put away the seven gods (cf. Jer. 4:1-2), thus recovering their mission identity as a light to the nations (cf. Isa. 42:6; 49:6). Only then does Yahweh become "indignant over the misery of Israel" (Judg. 10:16). Once again Israel encounters "the awesome fact of God's continued compassion in spite of their continual weakness" (Robert M. Polzin, *Moses and the Deuteronomist*, 161). There is grace abounding for the chief of sinners.

The Consequence of Repentance (10:17-18). The immediate consequence of putting away the gods of Ammon and other nations is an Ammonite "call to arms" (the Scribe uses the same Hebrew word in v. 12 for "cry") in order to crush any signs of independence among their formerly docile subjects. Besides crying to Yahweh, the leaders of Gilead look around for "the man that will begin to fight against the Ammonites" (v. 18). Apparently Ammonite power had either crushed or corrupted all potential leaders in Gilead during the eighteen-year occupation. The man of the hour was quietly biding his time in the borderland of Tob, like Moses in Midian (Exod. 3:1), David in Ziklag (2 Sam. 1:1), or Jeroboam in Egypt (1 Kgs. 11:40).

GOD'S DELIVERER

The Stone Which the Builders Rejected

The Scribe now pauses to introduce the future deliverer in seven quick strokes of the pen:

1. Jephthah's name ("God opens [the womb]") indicates that he will have a divinely appointed role to play, although when he opens his mouth he will close the womb of his virgin daughter (Judg. 11:35-36).

2. He is called "the Gileadite" three times (11:1, 40; 12:7). Despite the circumstances of his birth, he is a true native son of Gilead. Further, he is emphatically not an Ephraimite immigrant (cf. v. 4), but will arouse the envy of the Ephraimites (v. 1).

3. He is a skilled warrior (11:1), well qualified to lead the fight against the Ammonite oppressors. The Hebrew expression indicates that he has great courage like David ("a man of valor," 1 Sam. 16:18) and natural leadership ability like Jeroboam ("very able," 1 Kgs. 11:28).

4. He is the son of an extralegal liaison with "another woman" (Judg. 11:2), a "harlot" (v. 1). In Southeast Asian terms, she could be a minor wife, lover, or foreign woman, as in Neh. 13:23 (cf. Seth Erlandsson, "zānâ [zānāh]," *TDOT* 4:101). It is not clear whether this meant that Jephthah would be classified as a *mamzer* (RSV "bastard," NEB "descendant of an irregular union," NIV "born of a forbidden marriage") and therefore would be excluded from participation in the religious and political life of the community (Deut. 23:2). In any case, he was an outsider through no fault of his own.

5. He is the son of a nameless man of Gilead (the territorial name conceals the father's identity), who as a man of property would naturally have had to collaborate with the Ammonites in order to survive.

6. He is a disinherited fugitive from the envy of his half-brothers, who want above all to inherit his share of their father's property (Judg. 11:2). These envious half-brothers are also elders in Gilead (v. 7).

7. He is, finally, a kind of bandit chief of a group of dispossessed men ("worthless fellows") in the borderland of Tob. Eric J. Hobshawm has suggested that these might be escaped serfs, ruined freeholders, pastoralists denied access to sufficient pasturage, all of whom shared economic marginality. Jephthah would be "an outsider and a rebel, a poor man who refuses to accept the normal roles of poverty, and establishes his freedom by means of the only resources within reach of the poor, strength, bravery, cunning and determination" (*Bandits,* 76). In this role he resembles David (1 Sam. 22:1-2), who with his band extorted "protection money" from the rich, plundered Judah's traditional enemies, and shared the spoil with the village elders.

Tob, located near the sources of the Yarmuk River, was on the border separating Syrian, Ammonite, and Israelite power. It was, on the one hand, far from the corrupting influence of the occupying power but, on the other, in intimate contact with the gods of the nations. Tob remained outside the borders of Saul's kingdom. It was once allied with Ammon in a war against David (2 Sam. 10:6-8) but was later included in David's kingdom (Aharoni and Avi-Yonah, *The Macmillan Bible Atlas,* map 104).

113

The Head of the Corner

The dramatic meeting between the desperate elders of Gilead and their exiled kinsman in his border stronghold revolves around Jephthah's conditions for his return. When they offer to make him military commander ("leader," Judg. 11:6), Jephthah bargains further (v. 7), fearful that, with the victory won, he will be driven out again. The elders' second offer is to make him permanent "head over all the inhabitants of Gilead" (v. 8), which satisfies Jephthah's ambition to get back what he had lost (v. 9). This is guaranteed by an oath (v. 10) and confirmed in a religious ceremony at the Yahweh shrine in Mizpah (v. 11). The disinherited brother recovers his own inheritance in Mizpah of Gilead ("my house," v. 31). Jephthah's time has come to redress the wrongs of the past, and to take his rightful place as "*the* Gileadite."

LIBERATION: RECOVERY OF LAND

In this as well as other episodes in Judges, liberation means restoration of full rights to live on the land according to the Israelite "alternative notion of land tenure" as learned at Mt. Sinai (Walter Brueggemann, "Theses on Land in the Bible," 7). Power to administer the land must be taken away from the land-grabbers.

Whose Land?

At this point the Scribe introduces a lengthy debate between the king of Ammon and the messengers of Jephthah (Judg. 11:12-28). The purpose is to justify Israel's claim to the land which Ammon has been occupying and, following Israel's declaration of independence (10:16), is trying to annex outright by military force. In the first exchange (11:12-13), each claims the same piece of land as "my land." Such claims and counterclaims illustrate the fact that the Hebrew word *erets,* when translated as "land" in distinction from "earth," is "always conflicted, disputed, and at issue" (Brueggemann, "Theses on Land in the Bible," 5).

In the second exchange, Jephthah's messengers give a full explanation of Israel's claim (vv. 15-27). But the king of Ammon, speaking from a position of supposed strength, refuses to listen to any arguments (v. 28). It is this second exchange that illustrates Israel's theology of the land in a vivid way.

Yahweh, the Judge. This phrase at the end of the argument (11:27) states the Israelite presupposition for all land theology. Above all nations is the Judge (Ps. 82:8), who eventually "shall judge between the nations, and shall decide for many peoples" (Isa. 2:4; cf. Ps. 96:13; 98:9). This Judge is not indifferent to the ways of his nations (Ps. 86:9). At one time, he may decide to break a particular nation (Jer. 18:7) like "a potter's vessel" (Ps. 2:9). At another time, he may "build and plant" a nation (Jer. 18:9; cf. Isa. 40:24). Before this Judge all nations are equal, including Israel (Judg. 11:27).

Lands of the Nations. Jephthah refers to the lands of Moab (Judg. 11:15, 18), the Ammonites (v. 15), Edom (vv. 17, 18), and the Amorites (v. 21). These phrases reflect the belief that Yahweh has granted to each of the peoples an "inheritance" (Deut. 32:8). In Israel's worldview, the gods of the nations ("sons of God," Deut. 32:8; cf. Ps. 29:1 mg) were members of Yahweh's heavenly court (cf. Jer. 23:18, 22). They were assigned by the "judge of the earth" (Ps. 94:2) to particular nations (cf. Deut. 4:19) to look after their interests, order the life of that people on the land, and be accountable for their acts. A psalm from the period of the judges (Mitchell Dahood, *Psalms II.* Anchor Bible 17 [Garden City, N.Y.: Doubleday, 1968], 269) depicts the gods of the nations before a heavenly court, at which the great Judge asks them, "How long will you judge unjustly and show partiality to the wicked?" Then he commands them to "give justice to the weak and the fatherless; maintain the right of the afflicted and the destitute. Rescue the weak and the needy" (Ps. 82:2-4). Obviously the gods were not fulfilling their responsibilities in relation to the use of power and land.

Land of Israel. Yahweh was not only the Judge of all nations, but also "the God of Israel" (Judg. 11:21, 23). This term reveals a belief in a special relationship between the Judge of all nations, his people, and the land given them as a trust (Deut. 32:9; Josh. 1:2; Jer. 3:19). This may seem to some as a self-serving assumption of special privilege. A deeper look will show Israel as "a social experiment in the ancient world . . . an attempt to organize life outside of land monopoly" (Brueggemann, "Theses on Land in the Bible," 7). This radical kind of land tenure included the Jubilee regulation that the land should be returned to the original holders every forty-nine years, since it all belongs to Yahweh (Lev. 25:13), and the command against coveting what belongs to the neighbor (Exod. 20:17). Israel's mission identity (see above, pp. 60-61) involved this kind of land tenure policy. When Israel served the gods of other nations which were related to economic expansion, accumulation of wealth, and national security, their distinctive land policy was abandoned. Justice failed, and the poor suffered. Yahweh became angry.

Down to Cases. When the argument moves from theology to actual conflict over land claims, the picture becomes more clouded and ambiguous. The king of Ammon demanded that Israel "restore it [what is mine] peaceably" (Judg. 11:13), with the implied threat to seize it by force! This sounds like a diplomatic ploy by the powerful king to justify the action he had already planned to take (10:17; 11:4). His claim (v. 13) that Israel had earlier taken his land "from the Arnon [on the south] to the Jabbok [on the north] and to the Jordan [on the west]" was without foundation. Moab's northern boundary at the time of the Exodus was the Arnon (Num. 21:13), while Ammon's western boundary was Jazer (v. 24), close to Rabbath-ammon. Ammon's greed for Israel's land was the primary motive for this confrontation.

Israel's claim to the same piece of land was not based on an original grant from Yahweh, but rather on military conquest by which Yahweh had given them the land of the Amorites "from the Arnon to the Jabbok and from the wilderness to the Jordan" (Judg. 11:21-22). This was a grant to work out the implications of land tenure according to God's will. In this case, Israel was the aggrieved party trying to recover land given them by the Judge of the earth.

Yet there is the danger of smugness or even arrogance in the people's advice to the Ammonites to confine themselves to the area allotted them by Chemosh their (minor) god under Yahweh's jurisdiction, while Israel, the favorite of the Judge of all the earth, will take their war gains as a divine gift (v. 24). The argument that military victory implies divine approval can also serve as an excuse for the powerful to take more and thank God for it. Elijah's words to Ahab are relevant here: "Have you killed, and also taken possession?" (1 Kgs. 21:19; see below, pp. 123-24, "Perspectives," no. 3).

Victory by the Grace of God

The story resumes its dramatic action as soon as the Ammonite
king rebuffs the messengers (Judg. 11:28). In a spiritual contest
between Yahweh and the gods of Ammon (cf. Exod. 12:12),
Yahweh intervenes directly for the first time by causing his Spirit
to "come upon" Jephthah (Judg. 11:29), thus confirming the
appointment made by the elders (including Jephthah's brothers)
and people of Gilead (v. 11). The effect of this divine intervention
is (1) to inspire Jephthah to recruit militia in Gilead and north of
the Yarmuk River in East Manasseh (v. 29), and (2) to enable
Jephthah to win a decisive victory over the Ammonite king, thus
revealing the decision of the great Judge for Israel, against Ammon
and its gods (vv. 32-33).

Jephthah's Vow

The focus of the story of Jephthah is not so much on the victory
that he won with God's help as on his tragic vow which made the
victor a victim. Jephthah's vow from a troubled heart makes him
kin to those in all cultures who make vows. It is quite common in
Thailand, for example, for the visitor to a Buddhist temple to find
a play being performed by a professional troupe in fulfillment of a
vow made by the one sponsoring the drama. In Singapore puppet
plays sponsored in fulfillment of vows are often seen in the streets
at New Year's time.

In the Bible we find vows made to God as acts of unselfish
devotion (Ps. 132:2-5; Acts 18:18). Another form of vow is a
bargain with God that goes like this: If God will do thus-and-so
for me, I will do thus-and-so in response. Once God has carried
out his side of the bargain, the one who made the vow must do
what has passed his lips (Deut. 23:21, 23). Jephthah's vow was
such a bargain, like the vows made by Jacob (Gen. 28:20-22),
Israel (Num. 21:1-3), Hannah (1 Sam. 1:11), or Absalom
(2 Sam. 15:7-8; G. Henton Davies, "Vows," *IDB* 4:792-93).

Why Did He Make This Vow? Here is a reconstruction of the
event. On the night before the battle Jephthah, like Saul (1 Sam.
28:5, 8, 15), was deeply anxious about the outcome of the battle.
Some have speculated that his recruitment trip had not been

successful (John Gray, *Joshua, Judges, Ruth,* 318). A defeat would not only mean loss of land and independence for his people, but would be a personal disaster for Jephthah himself. Victory would mean everything to him personally. In the shrine at Mizpah, where he went to inquire of Yahweh, there was no word from Yahweh, either of promise as in the case of Joshua (Josh. 6:2; 8:1; 11:6) or of warning as in the case of Gideon (Judg. 7:2). Nor was there any sign, whether by fire (Judg. 6:21) or by nocturnal dew (vv. 36-40).

An Unnecessary, Unfaithful Act. Jephthah's deep sense of personal insecurity, which had been revealed in the encounter with his brothers and the other elders (11:4-11), showed itself again in his vow to Yahweh. This "mighty warrior" was not able to trust this God who maintained the awful silence. He was not able to live by his own challenge to the Ammonites to let Yahweh, "the Judge, decide . . . between the people of Israel and the people of Ammon" (v. 27). This points to the first problem with Jephthah's vow: it was unnecessary, since God had already given him the Spirit that should have assured him of victory. "If you refrain from vowing, it shall be no sin in you" (Deut. 23:22). There was no divine command, as in the case of Abraham (Gen. 22:2). Thus, Jephthah's vow was an act of unfaithfulness "desiring to bind God rather than embrace the gift of the spirit" (Phyllis Trible, *Texts of Terror,* 97).

"An Inhuman Sacrifice" (Trible, 93). The second problem with Jephthah's vow was that he promised to sacrifice a human being, a Canaanite practice specifically condemned by Israelite law (Lev. 18:21; 20:2). The laws frequently refer to the Canaanite custom of burning "their sons and their daughters in the fire to their gods" (Deut. 12:31; 18:9, 10). There is ample evidence that child sacrifice was indeed practiced in Israel (Ps. 106:37-38; 2 Kgs. 17:17). Micah spoke of giving "the fruit of my body for the sin of my soul" (Mic. 6:7) as a mistaken popular idea of "what is good." Jeremiah spoke often against child sacrifice (Jer. 3:24; 7:31; 19:4-6; 32:35), as did Ezekiel (Ezek. 16:20-21; 23:37-39). Kings of Israel were known to engage in this practice (2 Kgs. 16:3; 21:6; Charles F. Burney, *The Book of Judges,* 329-31; James L. Crenshaw, *A Whirlpool of Torment* [Philadelphia: Fortress, 1964], 11). [Note: despite the command to give "the first-

born of your sons" to Yahweh (Exod. 22:29), there was the further command to redeem the firstborn of humans by sacrificing an animal (Num. 18:15). Some scholars believe that human sacrifice was not forbidden in Jephthah's time. In the time of the Scribe, however, the law would have been well known.]

My Will Be Done. Another context in which to see Jephthah's vow is the borderland of Tob, where many cultures met and many gods were worshipped. This is no routine sacrifice of his firstborn son. Jephthah had no son, and he specifically states that the vow refers to "whoever comes forth from the doors of my house" (Judg. 11:31). The best analogy to this vow is the desperate act of the king of Moab, who offered "his eldest son who was to reign in his stead . . . for a burnt offering upon the wall," in order to avoid a humiliating defeat by Judah, Israel, and Edom (2 Kgs. 3:27). The prophetic word of Elisha (2 Kgs. 3:18-19) was thus overturned by a costly sacrifice. Jephthah was likewise trying to break the silence and force God's hand by his costly sacrifice. He was trying to demand of God that "my will be done," in order to assure himself of the victory and honor he so passionately desired (see below, p. 124, "Perspectives," no. 4).

Alas, My Daughter! The moment of glory and honor for the conquering hero is dramatically transformed by the joyful sound of timbrel and dance of a welcoming girl coming out of Jephthah's house. The trap set by the unnecessary, unfaithful, and impatient vow suddenly snapped shut on both father and daughter (cf. Prov. 26:27). Unlike the case of Jonathan (1 Sam. 14:43-45), there is no outcry from the newly liberated Gileadites to save the innocent victim or her grieving father. Unlike the case of Abraham (Gen. 22:12), there is no command from God to stay the father's knife or drown the cruel flames (see below, p. 124, "Perspectives," no. 5). Unlike the case of Absalom, there is no cry from the father, "Would I had died instead of you!" (2 Sam. 18:33). One of the few genuine tragedies in the Bible is played out as the father "did with her according to his vow which he had made" (Judg. 11:39; J. Cheryl Exum and J. William Whedbee, "Isaac, Samson, and Saul: Reflections on the Comic and Tragic Visions," 15, 30, 35).

In Memory of Her. The only redeeming feature of the tragic story of Jephthah's vow is the courageous self-sacrifice of his daughter. Her own lament on the mountains of Gilead (11:37-38) was not only to prepare herself for the death which would cut off her life in the prime of maidenhood, but to mourn the fact that her father would have no descendants to carry on his name and to maintain his inheritance which he had won back from his brothers.

The annual observance by "the daughters of Israel" was not to "lament" (RSV) but to "commemorate" (NEB, NIV) this woman's selfless deed. (The Hebrew word in v. 40 appears only once elsewhere in the OT, in 5:11, where it means to "recount" or "repeat" the triumphs of Yahweh and the people of Israel.) We may see the vow as an act of unfaith, but Jephthah's daughter accepted her father's interpretation that her life was the cost which had to be paid to secure the restoration of land to her people and leadership to her father. Her attitude, unlike her father's when he made the vow, was "not my will . . . but your will be done" (Luke 22:42 TEV). Thus we may apply the words of Jesus to this unnamed woman: "what she has done will be told in memory of her" (Mark 14:9). Unfortunately she has been forgotten by Scripture, which praises the father but makes no mention of the daughter (1 Sam. 12:11; Heb. 11:32; Trible, 107-8; see below, pp. 124-25, "Perspectives," no. 6).

Liberation Threatened

By artful design, the Scribe has described the unexpected outbreak of civil war which closes the story of Jephthah as an ironic replay of the liberation struggle against Ammonite aggression. Specific echoes of the earlier struggle are the call to arms (Judg. 12:1; cf. 10:17), the negotiations (12:1-3; cf. 11:12-28), Jephthah's question to his adversaries (12:3; cf. 11:12), and the great slaughter (12:6; cf. 11:33). The restoration of land and freedom wrought by victory over the oppressors is followed by bitter intertribal warfare.

Fire for Fire. The reason for this dramatic change is suggested by the interlude of the vow which separates the two episodes. Two themes of blood and fire link the vow with its sequel. With the reflected blaze from his innocent victim's pyre still on his face, Jephthah turns to confront a threat to make him a second but unwilling victim of the flames (12:1). Those who threaten to torch his house and burn him alive inside it are fellow Israelites from across the Jordan, ready to repeat the murderous example of Abimelech (9:49, 52). The grim warning of Jotham that fire begets fire (9:20) proves true, and portends future burnings (15:5-6; 18:27; 20:48).

Blood for Blood. Jephthah did not hesitate to shed the blood of his own daughter, nor did the Gileadites intercede to save her. Now Jephthah turns with great savagery to make the Jordan River run with the blood of the entire able-bodied male population of Ephraim (12:6; the census figures given in Num. 1:33; 26:37 are each less than the reported 42,000 Ephraimite casualties). The trivial cause that triggered this brutal overreaction was an insult (12:4) which sounds much more offensive in the Hebrew than it does in English (J. Alberto Soggin, *Judges,* 220). The derogatory description of the Gileadites by Ephraim and Manasseh contains an ironic sense which makes Jephthah the outcast leader of the outcasts. Communication breaks down: language, which should bind the two groups together (cf. Gen. 11:1), is now used to emphasize hostility and destroy unity (Judg. 12:5-6; cf. Gen. 11:9).

Ephraim apparently preferred a weak Gilead as a buffer between them and Ammonite power to an independent Gilead under a strong leader like Jephthah. They made a bid for hegemony in Transjordan by a crude threat on Jephthah's life (Judg. 12:1). When this did not work, they tried to shame the Gileadites, with disastrous results.

We do not hear of Gilead again until the all-Israel assembly at Mizpah in Ephraim (20:1). The tribes of Israel there order a savage raid on Jabesh-gilead (21:1-12). The present organization of the book of Judges suggests that this extermination of the population of that city, with the exception of four hundred young virgins, was a retribution for the death of Jephthah's virgin daughter and the subsequent slaughter of the Ephraimites at the Jordan ford (12:6).

If we take later evaluation seriously, despite his failings, Jephthah—like other deliverers of old—"conquered kingdoms" and "enforced justice" (Heb. 11:33) in Gilead for six years (Judg. 12:7). This was the shortest recorded period of any of the judges (not counting Abimelech, who was not a judge) and was only a third of the preceding period of oppression.

IBZAN, ELON, AND ABDON, THREE WISE ADMINISTRATORS

Judges 12:8-15

Timely Grace after Bloody Conflict

As the Scribe began the story of Jephthah with brief notes about two administrative judges (10:1-5), he now concludes it with three more. There is a certain symmetry among these five. Jephthah's tragic childlessness is paralleled by Tola (10:1-2) and Elon (12:11-12). No children are recorded for either of them. In contrast to Jephthah but like Gideon, Jair had thirty sons (10:4), while Ibzan had thirty sons and thirty daughters (12:9). Ibzan's home town of Bethlehem was in Zebulun (Josh. 19:15; not in Judah, cf. Judg. 17:7), in the valley of the Kishon River where the people of Zebulun fought so bravely against the forces of Sisera (4:10; 5:14, 18). We may conjecture that the levitical city of Nahalal/Nahalol (1:30; see above, pp. 45-46) may have been a teaching center for levitical priests during the brief judgeships of Ibzan and Elon.

Abdon, the fifth judge, balances Tola, the first of the five. Like Tola he lived in Ephraim near Shechem. Perhaps we may see in his forty sons and thirty grandsons a kind of replacement for Gideon's seventy sons who were murdered by Abimelech (9:5) and a new start for Ephraim, whose male population had been practically wiped out at the Jordan fords (12:6; see below, p. 125, "Perspectives," no. 7).

A final note about the length of service of the five. The forty-five years of the first two is reduced to twenty-five for the last three. This may reflect the Scribe's view of the deteriorating situation during the period of the judges.

PERSPECTIVES

1. Seven Spirits (see above, p. 110)

The seven groups of gods in this story remind us of Jesus' words about the evil spirit who "goes and brings with him seven other spirits more evil than himself, and they enter and dwell there; and the last state of that man becomes worse than the first. So shall it be also with this evil generation" (Matt. 12:45).

The reality of spirits is not doubted in many areas of the world. In a certain village in northern Thailand there has never been any response to the preaching of the Christian gospel. Evangelists say that the presence of a number of strong spirits is hostile to the liberating word there.

2. Gods of Nations Today (see above, p. 111)

Walter Wink has given a contemporary meaning to the gods of the nations as "the inner essence" or the "spirituality" of nations or other corporate entities, corresponding to their outer political, economic, military, or other structures and policies (*Naming the Powers*, 134-35; *Unmasking the Powers*, 87). Wink draws a line of continuity from the gods of the nations to the angels of the nations (Dan. 10:20-21), the "powers" referred to in the NT, and to the inner realities of power structures of today.

3. Land: A Burning Issue Today (see above, p. 116)

Ammon and Philistia (Judg. 10:7-8) correspond to powerful forces of today who, by political means (colonialism), economic domination (corporate finance), or projection of military might (spheres of influence), seek to control and exploit land and resources in such places as Central America, Afghanistan, and the Appalachian area of the United States.

Claims and counterclaims for the same area as "my land" (11:12-13) are heard today, for example in Burma where land claims are made against the central government by Karen, Kachin, Shan, and Chin tribal groups; in Sri Lanka by Sinhalese and

Tamils; in the Philippines by landowners and disinherited peasants; and on the Palestinian West Bank by Israelis and Palestinian Arabs.

The decision on each side of the negotiations to press for a decision by force of arms (11:12, 28) is also very contemporary. One side (Ammon) believed it had military superiority and could impose its will. The other side (Israel) believed its cause was just and relied on the God of justice and righteousness to give them the victory. Human perceptions of justice may be clouded by self-interest. The only solution is the one proposed by Jephthah: to place both sides under the judgment of a power higher than either.

4. Parents and Children (see above, p. 119)

Jephthah sacrificed his daughter because of his own anxieties and ambitions. Today parents who have a driving ambition to achieve security, wealth, or fame may, through neglect, unwittingly sacrifice the welfare of their own children. We might also look at nations whose drive for power or wealth or security is so strong that a whole generation of its youth may be lost in war, while aftereffects may lead many to drugs or crime.

5. God's Silence (see above, p. 119)

God's silence in this story reminds us that God does not always intervene to save us from the consequences of our foolish deeds. Even the gift of his Spirit (Judg. 11:29) does not protect us from rash words or deeds.

6. Jephthah's Daughter Remembered (see above, p. 120)

In Jewish legend Jephthah's daughter says, "I do not grieve for my death, not because I have to yield up my life, but because when my father vowed his heedless vow, he did not have me in mind." God responds that she is counted as wiser than her father and all the wise men, "and her death shall be precious before My face all the time" (Louis Ginzberg, *The Legends of the Jews* 4:44-45).

She appears in the Church of St. Catherine's Monastery on Mt. Sinai, along with Isaac, as a prefiguration of Christ's offering of himself as a sacrifice for the freedom of all on the Cross (cf. Harold L. Ginsberg, Nahum M. Sarna, and Bathja Bayer, "Jephthah").

7. Wise Administrators (see above, p. 122)

These five judges might be seen as dynamic equivalents of the holders of church and public office today. The "administrators" in Paul's list of the gifts of the Holy Spirit (1 Cor. 12:28) are primarily church leaders, "those . . . over you" (1 Thess. 5:12). Yet we know from the Bible that all good public administration is a gift of divine wisdom (Prov. 8:15-16), and that those outside the circle of faith still receive their authority from God (Rom. 13:3-4; 1 Pet. 2:13-14).

SAMSON,
THE PROFLIGATE JUDGE
Judges 13:1–16:31

The Saga

The Samson saga is the last of the six dramatic episodes which make up the main section of the Scribe's book of Judges. It is a lively human story of passion and love corrupted by fear, aggression, and bribery (Judg. 14:15; 16:5); of insult and retaliation (14:20; 15:3, 7, 10); of flaming fields and flaming death (15:4-6); of a hero who loves to look at women (14:1; 16:1), but is blinded because of his foolish love (v. 21); of a superman who can carry city gates 40 km. (24 mi.) uphill (v. 3) and burst unbreakable bonds four times, but who cannot break the bonds of a scheming lover; of a proud champion who twice is humbled and prays, once for life (15:18) and again for death, in order to accomplish his life's purpose (16:28, 30); of the mysterious workings of God in ways unrecognized by his own people (13:16; 14:4). Samson's great strength and tragic end have inspired poets, dramatists, and composers in a way that is not true of the other judges.

The Scribe indicates his own high evaluation of this last dramatic episode by the way he has preserved and enhanced the superb narrative art of the saga to produce its polished literary structure. Thus he invites the present-day reader to look beneath the surface for the theological message.

Note on the Saga as a Literary Form

For a description of saga, see James L. Crenshaw, *Samson*, 19-21. For a careful analysis of the structure, see J. Cheryl Exum, "Promise and Fulfillment: Narrative Art in Judges 13," 43-59; and "Aspects of Symmetry and Balance in the Samson Saga," 2-29. For the theological dimension, see James A. Wharton, "The Secret of Yahweh: Story and Affirmation in Judges 13–16," 48-66; and J. Cheryl Exum, "The Theological Dimension of the Samson Saga," 30-45.

The Context

We must read the Samson saga not just as an independent story, but in the context of the Scribe's book of Judges. It is the final episode in the double cycle of deterioration suggested in the theological essay (2:6–3:6; see above, pp. 59-60). Samson stands in sharp contrast to Othniel, the model judge of Judah for whom everything went well (3:7-11). Jewish tradition has seen him as the least worthy judge, the only one who fell into enemy hands and died in captivity (Myra Siff, Aaron Rothkoff, and Bathja Bayer, "Samson," 773).

As we have noted (see above, pp. 2-3), the wider context is the story which begins with creation and extends to the new creation in Jesus Christ. The author of the book of Hebrews has included Samson along with Gideon, Barak, and Jephthah among the "cloud of witnesses" who surround Christians (Heb. 12:1), the heroes of faith who "stopped the mouths of lions . . . were tortured . . . suffered mocking and scourging, and even chains and imprisonment . . . wandering . . . in dens and caves" (Heb. 11:32-38; cf. Judg. 14:6; 15:8; 16:21, 25).

OPPRESSION: THE FINAL TYRANNY

Of all the enemies of Israel in the book of Judges, the Philistines were the most persistent and, in the long run, most threatening. They posed a mortal danger to Israel up until their final defeat by David (2 Sam. 8:1). Behind the humor and pathos of the Samson saga lies this long-range threat to Israel's very existence as Yahweh's people and their witness to the covenant way of life over against the Canaanite way of death (see above, pp. 15-16).

The Philistines before Samson

"The regions of the Philistines" were not conquered by Joshua (Josh. 13:2). In the prologue to Judges the Philistines are the only adversary able to resist the victorious advance of Judah (Judg. 1:19; see above, pp. 34-35). "The five lords of the Philistines" head the list of nations left in Canaan to test and train Israel in the ways of war (3:3). Shamgar prevented the first pre-Philistine probe from the west (3:31). Likewise, the victory of Deborah and Barak prevented Sisera of the pre-Philistine Sea Peoples from another attempted incursion from the west. At the beginning of the Jephthah story we noted an unsuccessful attempt to establish an Ammonite-Philistine axis aimed at total control of trade routes in Canaan (10:7; see above, pp. 109-10). The beginning of the Samson saga (13:1) is a continuation of 10:6-8a, after a temporary digression to tell the story of the failure of the eastern end of the axis.

Philistine Double Identity

Demonic Tyrants. Two descriptions of the Philistines from the time of the Scribe suggest their double nature. First, they are called the "remnant of the Anakim" (Jer. 47:5 RSV, following Greek; Wilhelm Rudolph, *Jeremia,* 255), as the descendants of the fearsome gigantic tyrants who settled on the coast after Joshua drove them out of the Hebron area (Josh. 11:21-22). It had been necessary for Caleb to defeat a later generation of these Anakim again as a part of Judah's cleansing the land from Canaanite abominations (Judg. 1:10, 20; see above, p. 30). As descendants of the Anakim, the Philistines would seem almost demonic to the people of the Scribe's day.

Newcomers to Canaan. Second, the Philistines were known as "the remnant of the coastland of Caphtor" (Jer. 47:4). This identified them correctly as newcomers to the land of Canaan, like the Israelites under Joshua. Unlike the Israelites, however, they did not come as liberators but as the historical heirs of Egyptian imperial power in Canaan. Caphtor refers to the Aegean region (Jonas C. Greenfield, "Caphtor," *IDB* 1:534) from which the Philistines came (Amos 9:7; see above, p. 78) as one of the "Sea Peoples." They settled on the coast of Canaan during the reigns of Rameses II and Merneptah (1307-1225 B.C.E.; Frank M. Cross, *Canaanite Myth and Hebrew Epic,* 124) as vassals or mercenaries to serve as overseers of Egyptian imperial interests in

Canaan. They took over the Canaanite cities of Gaza, Ashkelon, and Ashdod, and built Gath and Ekron (which ruled over Timnah of the Samson stories) further inland for military and commercial control of the approaches to the hill country (Norman K. Gottwald, *The Tribes of Yahweh,* 411). When Egyptian power declined under Rameses III (1195-1164), the Philistines inherited the reins of power in Canaan for themselves. The Samson saga probably dates from this period of expanding Philistine ambitions (see below, p. 137, "Perspectives," no. 1).

Three factors made the Philistines such a mortal threat to Israelite independence: (1) their efficient political organization which made it possible for their five cities (Josh. 13:3) to act as one; (2) their military discipline; and (3) their superiority in military technology, including chariots (Judg. 1:19; 1 Sam. 13:5) and a monopoly on iron weapons which gave them an advantage over the bronze weapons of the Israelites (1 Sam. 13:19-21).

Note on the Term "Lords of the Philistines"

The Hebrew word translated as "lords" is the only surviving loanword from the otherwise unknown Philistine language. It refers to the military aristocracy which replaced the Canaanite ruling class. In this saga, they plot to destroy their national enemy Samson by discovering the secret of his strength (Judg. 16:5, 18). They rejoice in his humiliation (v. 23), but crash to their death around his head (vv. 27, 30).

GOD'S DELIVERER (13:1-25)

Judah's Long Silence

The story of the last judge begins in a way quite different from any of the other judges. In the Samson saga the period of oppression is twice as long as the previous longest oppression (13:1; cf. 4:3). Yet there is no cry of distress, no call for deliverance, no decision to renounce foreign gods and return to Yahweh (cf. 10:15-16). It appears that the people of Judah had accepted as unchangeable fate the fact that "the Philistines are rulers over us" (15:11).

Yahweh's Impatient Grace

The angel's word, "now therefore" (13:4 KJV; cf. Josh. 1:2), suggests a divine impatience, a critical turning point in God's view of things. If his people would not turn to him, he would take the initiative before it was too late. Zorah, the home of the pious but childless Danite couple (Judg. 13:2), was a mountain fortress guarding the valley of Sorek about 3 km. (2 mi.) from the Philistine border. The note that Yahweh was "seeking an occasion against the Philistines" (14:4) suggests the possibility that the Philistines planned to use this valley as a prime invasion route for the expansion of their economic and political power. A century later the Philistines followed the same route up through the Sorek Valley to the Rephaim Valley around Jerusalem in order to block David's rise to power (2 Sam. 5:18, 22; Yohanan Aharoni and Michael Avi-Yonah, *The Macmillan Bible Atlas,* map 100). A Philistine invasion of Judah in Samson's time would have been fatal for the emerging tribal federation.

Annunciation

God's final angelic intervention in the book of Judges does not carry a word of warning to his people against covenant breaking, as at Bochim (Judg. 2:1-5). God does not seek out a young man to empower as his deliverer, as in the case of Gideon (6:11-24). Instead, there is the announcement of a coming pregnancy and the birth of a baby boy who will begin the protracted struggle to deliver Israel from Philistine power (13:5). Samuel (1 Sam. 7:13), Saul (1 Sam. 9:16; 14:52), and David (2 Sam. 8:1) will complete the deliverance (see below, p. 137, "Perspectives," no. 2).

A Nazirite from Birth

Samson's words at the end of his life, when he is about to allow his hair to be shaved from his head (Judg. 16:17), sadly echo the angel's message to his mother, who adds the words "until the day of his death," with tragic overtones of the boy's end (13:5, 7). Samson had learned from his mother that he was to be "a Nazirite to God" (13:5, 7), meaning that he would be "holy" (Num. 6:5)

130

and specially consecrated to God (the meaning of Nazirite; Num. 6:2, RSV mg; see below, p. 138, "Perspectives," no. 3).

One of the many ironies of this story is that the Nazirite, who is not to drink wine or strong drink (Num. 6:4), himself puts on a drinking party at his wedding. (The Hebrew word translated "feast" in Judg. 14:10 means literally "drinking feast." "Strong drink" should probably be "beer"; Robert G. Boling, *Judges*, 219-20.) Then the holy man, who is not supposed to go near a dead body (Num. 6:6), scrapes out honey from a lion's carcass (Judg. 14:9) and certainly comes into contact with the bodies of the Philistines he killed (v. 19; 15:8, 15). Samson's character has always fascinated commentators. He has been called a bawdy giant, an obstreperous lout, a reckless irresponsible practical joker, a resistance hero, and a guerrilla fighter (see below, pp. 138-39, "Perspectives," no. 4).

Two Kinds of Faith

Traditional Faith. Manoah's faith is traditional and rational, but slow to recognize the presence of God. He follows correct procedures, first by setting about to check out his wife's story and to seek for details on how to bring up the boy (13:8). When he has confirmed the validity of her experience (v. 11), Manoah asks again for information about the meaning of their future son's life as one consecrated to God (v. 12). As custom demands, Manoah offers proper hospitality to his guest (v. 15), without realizing who he is (v. 16). He then tries to establish the stranger's identity by asking for his name (v. 17; rather like asking for a business card), in case anything goes wrong. Without getting a satisfactory answer to his questions, Manoah then makes an offering as though to hold Yahweh, "who works wonders," responsible for the words spoken by the stranger (v. 19). But when the angel ascends in the altar flame, Manoah is overcome with fear rather than awe, again according to traditional faith (v. 22; cf. Exod. 33:20).

Intuitive Faith. "The woman" (Judg. 13:3), on the other hand, has an intuitive faith. Sensing the supernatural character of the stranger, she accepts his words without asking details about his name or origin (v. 6), knowing in her heart that "God cannot be expressed but only addressed" (John Gray, *Joshua, Judges, Ruth,*

131

326). When the stranger makes himself visible (the literal meaning of the Hebrew word translated "appeared") a second time to her, she hastens to call her husband (v. 10). When the flame confirms her faith that the "man of God" was indeed the "angel of the LORD," she rightly counters her husband's fears with a faith in God's plan that occasions the seeing ("shown us") and the hearing of such wonderful things (v. 23).

Manoah's traditional faith would see Samson's life in a moralistic light as a story of broken vows, brutish behavior, the profligate wasting of a consecrated life, and a fatal weakness of the Danite man for Philistine women—as a negative example for the reader. Samson's mother would be more ready to see her son's life and death in relation to the "great deliverance" from the Philistines which he brings to one segment of the people of Israel (15:18).

LIBERATION

The Beginning of Liberation

Yahweh's Strange Blessing. Samson alone of all the judges is said to be blessed by Yahweh. Yet Yahweh's blessing does not carry its normal meaning of success in marriage, many offspring, long life, prosperity, or happiness. Blessing in Samson's case is quite specific. It gains him power to begin to save his people from the hand of the Philistines in the Sorek Valley. Although nothing in the Samson saga gives us grounds to believe it, the Scribe apparently considers that Yahweh's blessing also includes the ability to preside over twenty years of temporary peace along the Philistine border following the victory at Lehi (15:20). Samson's name means "sun," like the Assyrian name Shamshanu, or the Thai name Atit, or the Thai family name Suriwongse ("clan of the sun"). As the rising sun brings hope of a new day (cf. 5:31), so Samson's growth into young manhood with Yahweh's strange blessing on him (13:24) promises the dawn of hope for the eventual establishment of the united kingdom of Israel under David.

Yahweh's Strange Spirit. Behind the uncouth and violent behavior of Samson we find the relentless, impatient stirring of Yahweh's Spirit which would not let his consecrated one remain apart like an Indian *sadhu* or holy man who spends his life in the forest. The Spirit "began to drive him hard" (13:25 NEB; cf. Mark 1:12) into confrontation with his Philistine adversaries. It is between Zorah and Eshtaol (Judg. 13:25) that Yahweh's Spirit sets in motion a process which does not end until Samson's tortured body is brought up from Gaza to be buried in that very spot, in the tomb of his father (16:31).

The Spirit drives Samson down to Timnah (14:1; cf. Mark 1:12) to begin the drama of his wedding and its aftermath. On three subsequent occasions, the Spirit rushes on him with sudden power to tear apart a lion with his bare hands (Judg. 14:6; see below, p. 139, "Perspectives," no. 5), to kill thirty of Ashkelon's elite leaders (v. 19), to burst the bonds put on him by men of Judah in order to hand him over to the Philistines, and finally to kill another one thousand Philistines at Lehi (15:14-15). By implication the same Spirit gives him the strength to carry the gates of Gaza 40 km. (24 mi.) to Hebron (16:3), to break Delilah's bonds three times (vv. 9, 12, 14), and to bring the military, political, and social elite of Philistia to their death around his head (v. 30; see below, p. 139, "Perspectives," no. 6).

Samson's Three Strange Women

As in the opera *Tales of Hoffman* by Jacques Offenbach and Jules Barbier, the Samson saga revolves around the hero's adventures with three women. In each case there is an unexpected outcome. Samson's liaison with Philistine women from Timnah (14:1), Gaza (16:1), and the Sorek Valley (v. 4) recalls Joshua's warning against making marriages with "the remnant of these nations left here among you" (Josh. 23:12; cf. Deut. 7:3), as well as the wisdom teacher's warning against the "strange" or "foreign" woman" (Prov. 2:16 RSV mg). Jeremiah's words about the people of Judah of his and the Scribe's day also come to mind: "But you said, 'It is hopeless, for I have loved strangers [using the same word as in Prov. 2:16], and after them I will go'" (Jer. 2:25). The night spent with the harlot of Gaza recalls Hosea's words that Israel had "forsaken the LORD to cherish harlotry" (Hos. 4:10).

The saga's hero violates traditional teaching about relations with the other peoples and with their gods in the Promised Land, as

Manoah and his wife well knew (Judg. 14:3). We may guess that Samson's kind of behavior was not unusual along the border separating Judah, Dan, and Philistia. Hence the "Tales of Samson" would carry the fascination of taboo behavior by the hero who was obviously God's man. More than that, we are informed of what no one in the story knew, that Yahweh was actually supporting this unacceptable behavior as a secret way of blocking Philistine advance up the Sorek Valley (v. 4; see below, p. 140, "Perspectives," no. 7).

The Riddle of Samson's Life

Samson's encounter with the lion (14:5-9) not only gives him the idea for his riddle, but also breaks up his marriage (vv. 15-20) and provides four "occasions" against the Philistines (v. 19; 15:4, 8, 15). It also supplies a key to enable the discerning reader to understand the secret of the Samson story, which is itself a kind of riddle in which "God breaks the silence of eternity and couches his speech in mystery that conceals and invites interpretation" (Crenshaw, 107). The Samson saga is not a simple factual account but narrative art as retold by the Scribe in the latter days of the kingdom of Judah. We are invited to look for deeper levels of meaning.

Going Down to Timnah. First we should note that Samson is on his way down to Timnah with his parents to arrange for his risky wedding with the Philistine girl. He insists, against their better judgment, that she is "right in his eyes" (literal translation of the Hebrew expression "pleases me well," 14:3, 7). His repeated "going down" to Timnah (vv. 1, 5, 7, 10, 19), and later to Gaza (16:1, 21), means a fateful, deliberate entry into Philistine territory. From this perspective Samson is God's secret weapon.

The Vineyard. Suddenly Samson is alone, about to enter the Philistine (i.e., oppressors') vineyards of Timnah (14:5). In the setting of the impending wedding, the erotic associations of vine, vineyard, and wine spring to mind (Song of Sol. 1:2, 4; 2:13; 4:16; 5:1; 6:11; 7:2, 8-9, 12; 8:2), along with the warning that the grapes and wine of the enemy contain bitter poison (Deut. 32:32-33).

The vineyard reminds the reader of the Nazirite vow to "eat nothing that is produced by the grapevine, not even the seeds or the skins" (Num. 6:4), and anticipates Samson's drinking feast for the wedding party (Judg. 14:10). It also evokes thoughts of Isaiah's "Woe to the proud . . . drunkards of Ephraim," who "reel with wine and stagger with strong drink" (Isa. 28:1, 7). In a Greek drama, words of warning might be spoken by a chorus as the hero approaches the tempting vineyard.

The Lion. From this very vineyard a roaring lion leaps out at Samson. The terms "eater" (or "the devouring one"; cf. Jer. 2:30) and "the strong" (cf. 2 Sam. 1:23) of the riddle (Judg. 14:14) resonate with other verses about the wicked as a "ravening and roaring lion" (Ps. 22:13). Such a lion lurks in secret, watching for the hapless poor to drag him away (Ps. 10:8-9), with mouth open (22:21) and fangs bared (58:6), eager to tear his prey (17:12). Jeremiah spoke of the foe from the north, probably the Babylonians, as "a lion . . . a destroyer of nations" (Jer. 4:7). At this deeper level we may see the lion as a symbol for the contemporary enemy of Samson's time, namely the Philistines. Instead of finding love in the vineyards of Timnah, Samson encountered a murderous enemy. He was able to overcome the lion only by the power of God's Spirit!

The Honey. In the carcass of the dead lion Samson finds honey, eats it, and gives some to his parents. At first thought we might relate honey to erotic (Song of Sol. 4:11) but forbidden (Prov. 5:3) pleasures associated with the wine of the vineyard (cf. Song of Sol. 5:1). However, the honey is in fact associated with the dead lion. On one level, the honey may have served to revive Samson's strength and courage as in the case of Jonathan who, after his part in the great victory over the Philistines, ate some honey and "was refreshed" (1 Sam. 14:27, 29 NEB). At another level, honey would suggest a future period of peace after the destruction of the oppressing power when God would restore to his people the "land flowing with milk and honey" (Jer. 11:5; cf. Isa. 7:22) according to his promise. Giving the honey to his parents would be in effect encouraging them with hope that the whole affair of the wedding would turn out well for Israel in spite of the obvious dangers involved.

This incident ties together Samson's three affairs with Philistine women. In each case he *is looking for love* (symbolized by the vineyard). In each case he *meets danger* (symbolized by the lion).

His bride betrays him in order to save herself from death by fire at the hands of the young Philistine men at the wedding party (Judg. 14:15-18). The Philistines burn his wife and father-in-law in revenge for his burning of their crops (15:6), then seek to destroy him at Lehi (vv. 10, 14), and lay in wait for him again and again (16:2, 9, 12), until they are able to overcome, cripple, and humiliate him (v. 21).

In each case *a sudden onrush of strength* (the power of God's Spirit) enables Samson to overcome or outwit the enemy. In each case he *discovers an unexpected grace* (symbolized by the honey). Utterly exhausted after the deliverance brought by his victory at Lehi, he utters his humble prayer for deliverance from the hands of the Philistines (15:18). God's gift of water from the rock revives his strength and courage so that he is enabled to "judge" Israel for twenty years.

Divine grace in the last two incidents is more implied than expressed. Carrying the Gaza gates to Hebron is not only a gigantic effort, but it also brings hope for peace to the troubled land. As a descendant of Abraham, Samson has symbolically "possessed" the gates of the enemy with implied good news for all nations (Gen. 22:17-18). Depositing the gates "before Hebron" would be for the reader a hidden clue to David's coming victory over the Philistines (see above, p. 30). Finally, when he has become the blinded, powerless victim instead of the powerful victor, Samson finds hope again in the growth of his hair (Judg. 16:22). Once again he utters a prayer asking for a return of blessing and strength, offering his own life as a sacrifice. Listeners to the saga knew that he would bring down the leadership of the Philistines and that his death would promise peace in the land of milk and honey (see below, p. 140, "Perspectives," no. 8).

The Deeper Meaning of the Riddle. The riddle, on its face a bawdy or ribald wedding night joke among male companions, carries deeper meanings. Out of the "eater" (the shambles of the old destructive order) comes "something to eat": the hope of *shalom*, of milk and honey in the Promised Land of the future. Out of the "strong" (the broken political, economic, and military machine) comes something "sweet": "a land of olive trees and honey, a land . . . in which you will lack nothing" (Deut. 8:8-9), where there will be the sweetness of God's word as the guide to peace (Ps.

19:10; 119:103) and "pleasant words . . . like a honeycomb," bringing "sweetness to the soul and health to the body" (Prov. 16:24). The real meaning of this honey of new life and hope for a better future is discovered not by the proud, but by those who acknowledge their own need, humbly call on the Giver of life (Judg. 15:18), and offer their lives for the accomplishment of his purposes of *shalom* (16:30).

PERSPECTIVES

1. Two Views of the Enemy (see above, pp. 128-29)

In time of war or severe tension, the simpler demonic view which sees the enemy as absolutely evil ("remnant of the Anakim, " Jer. 47:5) is predominant. Calmer heads will prefer the other view which looks at the adversary as subject to historical forces, fears, and ambitions like all nations, while not minimizing the seriousness of the threat. Interestingly, two biblical passages reflect the second view of the Philistines. Amos said that Yahweh called them from Caphtor, just as he had called the Israelites from Egypt, thus placing both within the circle of divine love (Amos 9:7). Psalm 87:4 expresses the belief that one day Philistia will become a member of God's family of nations, redeemed and reborn by their knowledge of God.

2. Chosen from the Womb (see above, p. 130)

The annunciation story (Judg. 13) puts Samson in a surprising company of others similarly chosen by God: Ishmael, that "wild ass of a man" (Gen. 16:11-12); Isaac (Gen. 18:10), who like Samson offered himself as a sacrifice (22:9); Immanuel, who was a sign that God would intervene to save his people (Isa. 7:14); Jeremiah (Jer. 1:5), who like Samson was opposed by his people (v. 19) and died in captivity (43:5-7); the "Servant of the LORD" (Isa. 49:5), who like Samson was blind and disfigured (42:18-19; 52:14); John the Baptist (Luke 1:13), who also died in captivity (9:9); Jesus, who by his death would also "save his people" (Luke 1:31; Matt. 1:21); and Paul (Gal. 1:15), who was bound in prison with chains and died in captivity (Acts 26:29).

3. Parallels with Asian Customs (see above, pp. 130-31)

The *hair of the head* is widely seen as a sacred part of the body. The Thai word used for the first person masculine pronoun is *pom*, which means "hair" or more specifically, "topknot." Like the Sikhs of India, Samson did not cut his hair (Judg. 13:5; Num. 6:5). Buddhist *bikkhus* (monks) in Thailand observe the opposite custom of shaving the hair of the head and eyebrows as a way of separating themselves from ordinary men (cf. Num. 6:18, where shaving off the hair from one's head is a sign of return to ordinary life). The Nazirite *dietary restrictions* against wine find their counterpart in those of the *bikkhus*, who must refrain from alcoholic beverages and meat, and those of Thai spirit mediums, who must not eat anything that is harvested from the ground, such as roots or ground nuts. Contamination by contact with dead bodies (Num. 6:6-7) is also forbidden to some classes of holy persons in Asia. Like the Nazirites (Num. 6:5, 13-20), *bikkhus* may take up their vows for a limited period of time and then return to ordinary life. Samson, on the other hand, was consecrated "from birth to the day of his death" (Judg. 13:7). The kind of *marriage custom* reflected in Samson's marriage resembles that in North Thailand, where the groom goes to live in the bride's family home after the wedding.

4. Was Jesus a Nazirite? (see above, p. 131)

The Greek of Matt. 2:23 identifies Jesus as a "Nazorean" (NAB; other versions change the reading to "Nazarene"; cf. RSV). Some early Christians compared him to Samson the Nazirite, because of the similarity between the words of the angels to the mothers of Samson and Jesus (Judg. 13:3; Luke 1:31; see Raymond E. Brown, *The Birth of the Messiah* [Garden City: Doubleday, 1979], 210-25). According to Frederick W. Danker, Matthew presents Jesus as a second Samson who comes to deliver his people. Danker sees a further correspondence between the ridicule endured by Samson and the mocking of Jesus, and in the salvific effect of the death of each (*Multipurpose Tools for Bible Study*, 92). The Nazirite vow must have been the background for the description of John the Baptist: "He shall drink no wine nor strong drink" (Luke 1:15; cf. 7:33). On the other hand, Jesus, who came "eating and

drinking" and was "a friend of . . . sinners" (Luke 7:34), was more
like Samson.

5. *Samson: A World Hero (see above, p. 133)*

Samson's bare-handed fight with the lion makes him a world hero.
In Israelite tradition, David recounts his encounter with a lion
while he is preparing for his contest with the Philistine giant
Goliath (1 Sam. 17:34-35). Benaiah, one of David's mighty men,
did the same (1 Chron. 11:22). The mythological Babylonian
heroes Gilgamesh and Ilu-shamash (Charles F. Burney, *The Book of
Judges,* 400-401) and the Greek hero Heracles (George F. Moore,
Judges, 364) are also said to have slain lions. Some have suggested
that these models may have affected the telling of the Samson saga.
Medieval Christian art pictured Samson rending the lion in a way
that compares him to Jesus overcoming Satan and breaking the
jaws of hell (Siff, Rothkoff, and Bayer, 773). One early church
father, Ephraim Syrus, saw the lion as the image of death, and
honey as "the sweetness of life" (*Hymns on the Nativity* ix).
Another, Ambrose, saw the honey coming from the lion's body as
"grace . . . from the offence, power from weakness, and life from
death" (*On the Holy Spirit* ii.8).

6. *God's Spirit (see above, p. 133)*

The violent effect of God's Spirit on Samson (Judg. 14:6, 19;
15:14) reminds us of Jesus' description of John the Baptist as a
man "of violence" who takes the Kingdom of Heaven "by force"
(Matt. 11:12; cf. George Arthur Buttrick's remark that "a Samson-
strength" comes to those whom Christ calls to do spiritual battle
["The Gospel According to St. Matthew: Exposition," *IB* 7:383]).
Samson reminds us that God uses different kinds of people to
accomplish his purpose. We learn from other references about
different manifestations of God's Spirit (Isa. 11:2; 42:1; 61:1;
Mark 1:10, 12; Gal. 5:22-23).

7. Love Corrupted (see above, p. 134)

The corruption of the marriage relationship by economic and social factors, as we see in Samson's marriages, mirrors our own time. A shocking example of this corruption lies behind a law passed by the Indian Parliament outlawing dowries. This law seeks to prevent the practice of burning brides to death in some kind of "accident" should the bride not bring as much property as the groom's family would desire. In the outlawed practice, the dowry would remain with the groom's family, and the groom could, after the "accidental" death of the bride, seek another wife with a larger dowry.

8. A Samson Syndrome (see above, p. 136)

An Israeli Jew recently expressed concern about what he called "a Samson syndrome" among some Israelis, who would be willing to take the entire Arab world with them into the abyss of annihilation rather than accept any accommodation with Palestinian Arabs as neighbors (Yehezkel Landau, *Jerusalem Post*, 11 August 1985). The same attitude threatens our whole world in an age when nuclear war would mean "mutually assured destruction" (MAD).

PART III
THE EPILOGUE:
AFTER THE JUDGES

Judges 17:1–21:25

ABOMINATIONS IN THE PROMISED LAND

Judges 17:1–21:25

The epilogue brings the early history of the people of God "at risk in the Promised Land" to a further descent into evil. Taken by itself, the book ends as a tragedy in which the hero's (Israel's) flaws bring ultimate destruction. The angel's words at Bochim (Judg. 2:2), the prophet's words in Manasseh (6:10), and Yahweh's words in Gilead (10:13) are fulfilled in these two narratives which close the book of Judges. It is only in the larger perspective of the biblical drama that we can see God's timely grace.

The Locus of Abominations: The Hill Country of Ephraim

It is not by chance that the Scribe places the final scenes of this narrative in the hill country of Ephraim (17:1; 19:1). Here the ambiguity of the early history of Israel is focused. Ephraim was the heartland of the northern tribal territories. It was made holy by the graves of Joshua (2:9), Tola (10:2), and Abdon (12:15). Ephraim's freedom, won by Ehud (3:27), Shamgar (3:31), and Deborah (4:5), had enabled them to create new and wider areas of political unity out of the fragmented Canaanite city-state system, and to develop the Israelite legal tradition initiated by Moses (see above, p. 45).

This freedom had a darker side. In Shechem, just north of Ephraim's border, the blood of Abimelech's victims had cried out for vindication against the tyrant (9:24). Ephraim's jealous inter-tribal rivalry brought bloody civil war to the tribes (8:1-2; 12:1-6). As these episodes unfold, we can hear the sad tones of the "litany of lament" from the prologue and sense a melancholy anticipation of the fall of the northern kingdom (1:29; see above, p. 43, and see below, p. 156, "Perspectives," no. 1).

The First Cause of Abominations: A Leadership Vacuum

The statement that there was "no king in Israel" appears four times in the epilogue (17:6; 18:1; 19:1; 21:25). The Scribe thereby implies a lack of strong sustained moral and political leadership which would serve to bind the confederation of tribes together. Such leadership would make them strong enough to withstand the growing threat of the Philistines in the period between Samson, the last of the judges, and Samuel the king-maker. The statement must be qualified to read that there was in the Scribe's view as yet "no [true] king in Israel" (i.e., in contrast to the canaanized king Abimelech) who would restrain intertribal rivalries and protect the rights of the poor (see above, pp. 27-28).

The true king anticipated by the Scribe must be the one described in Deut. 17:14-20, who keeps a copy of the Torah ("this law") with him and reads it every day as his own guide to doing "right and good in the sight of the LORD" (Deut. 6:18). Such a king would make "righteousness flourish, and peace abound," and make people "blossom forth from the cities like the grass of the field" (Ps. 72:7, 16). In the time of the Scribe, Josiah had been such a king; he "did what was right in the eyes of the LORD, and walked in all the way of David his father" (2 Kgs. 22:2), and did "justice and righteousness" (Jer. 22:15). Josiah's tragic death in 609 B.C.E. brought his righteous reign to an end.

This perspective helps us to understand the Scribe's negative view of the kingship implied in Gideon's refusal to rule over his people (Judg. 8:23; see above, p. 99) and expressed by Gideon's son Jotham (9:7-21; see above, p. 102). What is condemned here is a particular kind of kingship dominated by political Baalism. The prime example in Judges of a perverted kingship is Gideon's son Abimelech. In the time of the Scribe, the practitioner of political Baalism was Josiah's son Jehoiakim, who had "eyes and heart only for . . . dishonest gain, for shedding innocent blood, and for practicing oppression and violence" (Jer. 22:17).

The Second Cause of Abominations: Unbridled Self-Interest

In the epilogue the Scribe shows us a society liberated again and again from external oppression, finally sinking into moral anarchy

144

and social chaos. Self-interest was the only value left, and this meant relegating all other values into a value-free relativism. Everyone did "what was right [Heb. *yashar*] in his own eyes" (Judg. 17:6; 21:25), without regard to God's will for the nation. It was the perversion of the purpose of creation, as seen by the wisdom writer: "God made man upright [*yashar*], but they have sought out many devices" (Eccl. 7:29). Moses warned the people against "every man doing whatever is right in his own eyes" before the people entered the Promised Land (Deut. 12:8; see below, p. 156, "Perspectives," no. 2).

THE FIRST ABOMINATION: IDOLATRY

Judges 17:1–18:31

From Bethel to Dan

In this narrative, the idols are made at Micah's home and are carried north to Dan. Robert G. Boling's proposal ("Levitical History and the Role of Joshua," 247) that Micah's home was in or near Bethel suggests the possibility that this episode of the epilogue balances the Bethel incident of the prologue (see above, p. 39). Both sections begin with Bethel and end with Dan. The story of the northern tribes, which occupies most of the central section of Judges, begins in the prologue at the canaanized shrine city of Bethel, rebuilt from the ruins of Luz, and ends in the first part of the epilogue at the canaanized shrine city of Dan.

The Idols: Key to the Story

The first episode in the prologue revolves around several images and focuses on the problem of idolatry. At the beginning (Judg. 17:3, 5) we witness the making of a "graven image and a molten image" (possibly a single image of carved wood or stone covered with metal) for Micah's private shrine. The story ends with a "graven image" installed in the rebuilt shrine city of Dan (18:30-31). Micah also made "an ephod and teraphim" (17:5). The Scribe underlines the key importance of these images by repetition. The molten image, ephod, and teraphim are mentioned five times each, while the graven image appears eight times.

The story is told in a very matter-of-fact manner, as though there were nothing unusual about the fact that Micah the Ephraimite made and used such images or that a tribe of the Yahwist confederation set them up in their tribal shrine. On the

146

other hand, if we read this narrative through the eyes of the implied readers during the reign of Jehoiakim when idolatry was rife (cf. Jer. 7:17-18), the images would appear in a different light, as portents of a coming disaster. A century earlier the northern kingdom had fallen to Assyria because of the idolatry prevailing there.

Two of these cultic objects have appeared before in Judges, each in a pivotal role. First, the "graven image" (Heb. *pesel*) has appeared in the Ehud story, there translated "sculptured stones," in key positions at the beginning and end (Judg. 3:19, 26; see above, pp. 71, 75). There they are symbols of foreign domination, signifying that the land and people belong to Molech rather than to Yahweh. In the Micah story, the "graven image" symbolizes not foreign oppression but internal alienation from the God of the covenant.

Second, Micah's ephod turns the reader's attention to Gideon's ephod made of plundered ornaments from the Midianite oppressors. Regardless of the original intention of Gideon, this cultic object led all Israel to fall under the seductive influence of the gods of Canaan (8:27; see above, pp. 100-101). The reader is led to a similar conclusion in the case of Micah's ephod, except that the idols precede the construction of the ephod. This suggests that Micah had already succumbed to the gods of Canaan through the influence of his mother.

Beyond the book of Judges, the four cultic objects appear in contexts which suggest a continuing struggle against their use. A very early curse lay upon the one "who makes a graven or molten image, an abomination to the LORD, a thing made by the hands of a craftsman, and sets it up in secret" (Deut. 27:15). The Mosaic law expressly forbade the manufacture of these objects (Exod. 20:4; Deut. 4:16, 23, 25).

Both the ephod and teraphim were closely related to royal power (cf. Hos. 3:4) and doing "what is right" in the eyes of the king. At the king's command (cf. 1 Sam. 23:9), priests would manipulate the ephod or teraphim to communicate with God, something like the court Brahmins in the Thai royal establishment. The problem was that the king might get the very reply *he* wanted instead of a word from *God* (cf. 1 Kgs. 22:6, 12). For this reason, Samuel called the use of teraphim "idolatry" (1 Sam. 15:23; so

translating Heb. *teraphim*), using it in parallel with the word
"divination." In later years a prophet would call any information
gained by the use of the teraphim "nonsense" (Zech. 10:2).
Jehoiakim's father Josiah removed the teraphim from the land of
Judah along with other idols in order to restore the authority of
God's teaching *(torah)* in the land (2 Kgs. 23:24).

We can only speculate about the kind of images implied in this
story. We might guess that the first was a graven image of Asherah,
the Canaanite fertility-goddess. We learn from the theological essay
(Judg. 2:13) and the Gideon episode (6:25-30) that the cult of
Asherah was part of the corrupting influence of the gods of
Canaan. On the assumption that Micah's mother was a devotee
of this cult, she would be like the deposed queen mother of King
Asa (1 Kgs. 15:13), or like Queen Jezebel, who kept four hundred
prophets of Asherah in her employ (18:19). King Ahab (1 Kgs.
16:33) made an Asherah, and King Manasseh even placed his
graven image of Asherah in the Jerusalem temple (2 Kgs. 21:7).
King Josiah purged these images from the temple (2 Kgs. 23:4-7,
15) in accordance with the law (Exod. 34:13; Deut. 7:5; 12:3).

The "molten image" may have been a small representation of
a young bull, the Canaanite symbol of male virility (cf. Judg. 6:25),
like the golden calf made by Aaron at Mt. Sinai/Horeb (Ps.
106:19) or the two molten images made by Jeroboam and placed
in Bethel and Dan (1 Kgs. 12:28-29; cf. Hos. 13:2), where they
remained until the end of the northern kingdom (2 Kgs. 17:16).

The Widow's Idolatrous Search for Security

Four kinds of idolatry appear in this narrative, represented by the
four main actors: Micah's mother, Micah, the Levite, and the
Danites. In each case the idols are central (see below, pp. 156-57,
"Perspectives," no. 3).

The Insecurity of Widowhood. Micah's mother was presumably a
widow, since no husband is mentioned. In the society of that time
she had to bear the "reproach" or disgrace of widowhood (Ruth
1:20-21; Isa. 54:4). Widows were particularly vulnerable to exploitation or oppression (cf. Isa. 10:1-2). Like the other four
mothers who appear prominently in Judges, Micah's mother is
nameless. Unlike the mothers of Abimelech (Judg. 8:31) and

Jephthah (11:1), but like Sisera's mother (5:28), she was a person of some wealth and social standing. Her eleven hundred pieces of silver above and beyond her other resources puts her in an economic class equal to the Philistine military elite (16:5) and invites comparison with the wealthy women of Israel in a later time who got their wealth by exploiting the poor (cf. Amos 4:1; Isa. 3:16-23). The size of her wealth contrasts with the yearly allowance of ten pieces of silver which Micah gave to his priest (Judg. 17:10). The houses (18:14) in the walled compound with its own gate (v. 17) in which Micah and his family, his mother, and the priest lived also speak of wealth (Norman K. Gottwald, *The Tribes of Yahweh*, 291). Her vulnerability is suddenly visible again when her own son steals her savings.

Idolatrous Security. Unlike Samson's mother with her simple intuitive faith (ch. 13; see above, pp. 131-32), this mother's relationship to God is calculating and cynical. True, she gave her son a Yahwistic name ("Micah" means "Yahweh the incomparable"), pronounced a blessing (and presumably her curse) in the name of Yahweh (17:2), and consecrated the silver to Yahweh (v. 3). Yet the Scribe is careful to point out that she not only shrewdly reversed her curse when she saw that the thief was her son (v. 2), but also kept back most of the consecrated silver for herself and had the rest made into images of silver (v. 4; cf. Isa. 2:20). The graven and molten images were her way of overcoming her vulnerability as a widow. By giving them to her son to place in the family shrine, she hoped to bind her security to that of her son. Ironically, by involving her son in her idolatrous search for security she was guilty before God of "enticement" to serve other gods (cf. Deut. 13:6-7).

Security Lost. The emptiness of a security based on idols became clear when the Danites stole the idols she had given to Micah.

Micah's Idolatrous Search for Prosperity

According to the meaning of Micah's name, he should have been a man of faith. Ironically, in this narrative he is obsessed with securing his own prosperity by employing a priest and putting his trust in idols.

Prosperity Aborted. Micah became instantly prosperous by his theft of his mother's wealth (Judg. 17:2). In this act of unfaith, he is like Achan, who also coveted and "took" a much smaller amount of silver (Josh. 7:21). Micah prefigures the deep sickness of society in the Promised Land in the days of Hosea (Hos. 4:2) and Jeremiah (Jer. 7:9). He returned the stolen treasure not out of repentance for an evil deed, not out of sympathy for his widowed mother, but because of his fear of the effects of his mother's curse on him. He had failed in his first search for prosperity.

Prosperity Guaranteed. After Micah had appointed the Levite as priest, he revealed his true motive: "Now I know that the LORD will prosper me, because I have a Levite as priest" (Judg. 17:13). In this remark, Micah's purpose in employing a priest and using the idols is clear: to guarantee prosperity, though without any corresponding demands on him for obedience. Although he believed that Yahweh would grant this prosperity, he later called the idols "my gods which I made" (18:24). The narrator refers to them as "what Micah had made" (v. 27) and "Micah's graven image which he made" (v. 31). Micah is portrayed as a god-maker in a day when Jeremiah's challenge would have echoed in the ear of the reader: "Can man make for himself gods? Such are no gods!" (Jer. 16:20; see below, p. 157, "Perspectives," no. 4).

Prosperity Lost. Micah began his idolatrous search for prosperity by stealing his mother's wealth. The search ended when the Danites stole his gods and his priest. With the loss of his cultic apparatus nothing was left of his religion. Micah's predicament, which resonates to Yahweh's argument in the time of Jephthah (Judg. 10:14), finds an echo in Jeremiah's taunt to Judah: "Where are your gods that you made for yourself? Let them arise, if they can save you, in your time of trouble" (Jer. 2:28; cf. Judg. 10:14). Gods which can be stolen away are in reality no gods at all.

The Levite's Idolatrous Search for Position

The ideal role of the Levites was to serve as the representatives of the people in public and national worship, to symbolize and re-establish the sanctity of the holy nation, and to maintain the covenant relationship with God on behalf of the nation (Raymond Abba, "Priests and Levites," *IDB* 3:877-78). The Levite in this narrative appears as an opportunist who will do anything to get a better position for himself and his descendants.

A Sojourner without Position. Whereas in Joshua the Levites were given permanent living places (the levitical cities) with their own means of livelihood (Josh. 21:3), the Levite in this narrative is a vulnerable temporary resident among people who were not his blood relatives. The Hebrew verb *gur* describes his temporary residence in Bethlehem (Judg. 17:7, "sojourn") and his purpose in going to the hill country of Ephraim (v. 8, "live"; v. 9, "sojourn"). Again we note the contrast. In Joshua, the Levites, because they have no tribal territory, could serve as independent interpreters of Covenant Teaching and stress supratribal loyalties. In Judges, the nontribal character of the Levite makes him dependent on the hospitality of anyone who will give him a place to live and "fill his hand" (the literal meaning of the verb translated "install" in vv. 5, 12).

Position Achieved. The Levite found his desired position in the employ of Micah. Instead of acting as Yahweh's representative in interpreting Covenant Teaching, he was more like the priests described by the prophet Micah who plied their trade "for hire" (Mic. 3:11; cf. Judg. 18:4: "He has hired me, and I have become his priest"). He could be hired to give a word from God (v. 5). By carefully omitting any statement that the Levite actually did inquire of Yahweh, the Scribe implies that his reply to the scouts was his own, not God's. His comforting words, "go in peace" (v. 6, where "peace" means "victory" as in 8:9), were the basis for the scouts' assurance that "God has given it [the land of Laish] into your hands" (18:10). The irony of priestly encouragement would not be missed by a reader in the seventh century B.C.E., when prophet and priest were plying their trade (Jer. 14:18) and saying, "'It shall be well [*shalom*] with you'; and to every one who stubbornly follows his own heart . . . 'No evil shall come upon you'" (Jer. 23:17).

The Levite made the best use of his role as one who could guarantee prosperity to his patrons (cf. Judg. 17:13) by accepting a more attractive job offer from the Danites. The Scribe's three comments (18:20) tell volumes: (1) His "heart was glad," with no suggestion of loyalty to Micah, or any effort to consult with Yahweh. (2) He took with him the cultic apparatus, thus blessing

151

the Danites' theft of these things from Micah and showing the importance of the idols in his profession. (3) He "went in the midst of the people," thus leading them into idolatry, ready to bless them at every step of their campaign.

Position Lost. The Scribe reserves the final note of irony to the end. The anonymous wandering Levite ready to ply his trade for the highest bidder turns out to be a direct descendant of Moses (18:30)! The phrase "until the day of the captivity" clearly implicates this priesthood in the worship of the molten image of the golden bull which Jeroboam I had placed in the Danite sanctuary (1 Kgs. 12:29-30) and which was a cause of the downfall of the north (2 Kgs. 17:16). The Levite's idolatrous search for priestly position led to the disasters of 732 and 722, giving an ominous color to the Levite's ambiguous blessing, "The journey on which you go is under the eye of the LORD" (Judg. 18:6; cf. Prov. 5:21).

Note on the Levites in Judges 17–21

Two Views of the Levites. The picture of a wandering, unemployed Levite, seeking to "find a place" to live and work (Judg. 17:8, 9), contrasts sharply with the dominant role of the Levites in Joshua (see E. John Hamlin, *Inheriting the Land,* 140-44). One way to explain this contrast is to identify materials drawn from different periods of Israelite history in these two presentations (Boling, "Levitical History and the Role of Joshua," 247-49). This does not help us to understand why the two authors used the available material in such different ways. It is perhaps more fruitful to look at the different situations which lie behind the two books as we have them.

The Levites in Joshua and Deuteronomy. One way of looking at the book of Joshua is to see it as the author's interpretation of the past and his proposal for the reconstruction of society resulting from the reform movement under King Josiah (Hamlin, *Inheriting the Land,* xiii-xvi). The author of Joshua saw Levites as the guardians of the sacred Mosaic teachings and hence the best protection against the temptations of Baalism in the Promised Land. The teaching and commands of Moses are very prominent in Joshua, as is shown by the fifty-nine occurrences of the name. Indeed, the forty-eight levitical cities (Josh. 21) should be understood as a symbolic plan to allow this teaching to penetrate all aspects of the life of each tribe (Hamlin, *Inheriting the Land,* 140-56). The role of the levitical priests in Joshua corresponds to their role as portrayed in Deuteronomy (Deut. 10:8; 31:9). In addition, the author of Deuteronomy saw them as the keepers and interpreters of the Covenant Teaching for the true king.(Deut. 17:18-19).

The Levites in the Post-Joshua Generation. The Scribe, living in the time of Jehoiakim, pictures the Levites as a part of the generation(s) after Joshua "who did not know the LORD" (Judg. 2:10; see above, p. 59) and who repeatedly "did what was evil in the sight of the LORD, forgetting the LORD their God, and serving the Baals and the Asheroth" (3:7). In sharp contrast to Joshua, the name Moses is almost absent from Judges. In the prologue, "the commandments of the LORD, which he commanded their fathers by Moses" (3:4), are the standard by which subsequent behavior is to be judged. In the epilogue (18:31), a levitical descendant of Moses presides over the worship of the graven image forbidden by those very commandments! (The only other references to Moses in 1:20 and 4:11 give historical information not relevant to the role of the Levites.)

Jeremiah's View of the Priesthood. The most probable background for the Scribe's view of the failure of the Levites is the condition of the priesthood during the reign of Jehoiakim. We learn from Jeremiah that the priests who should have led the people in the way of Covenant Teaching did not know Yahweh (Jer. 2:8). They worshipped wood and stone images (Jer. 2:26-27). Instead of leading the people to God's ways and will, they told the people just what they wanted to hear, parroting the lying words of the false prophets (Jer. 5:31). In one famous incident, the priests helped to stir up a mob spirit to murder Jeremiah when he spoke of the coming destruction of Jerusalem (Jer. 26:7-9).

A Restored Priesthood. In contrast to this negative view of the priesthood by Jeremiah, we also find that the prophet had a firm hope for the future role of the levitical priests. They would be true interpreters of the Covenant Teaching for the messianic descendant of David in the age to come (Jer. 33:18-22). This view of the Levites playing their true role by the side of the Davidic messiah corresponds to what we have seen in Joshua and Deuteronomy.

The Danites' Idolatrous Search for Land

Land is the major theme of Judg. 18. The Hebrew word *erets* appears ten times, translated as "land" (Judg. 18:2, 9, 10, 17, 30), "earth" (vv. 7, 10), or "country" (v. 14). Words and expressions used in this climactic part of the narrative suggest an ironic parallel with the Exodus and Conquest narratives. The irony is this: it is an Exodus journey without Sinai, a land conquest without covenant. Instead of Sinai there is Micah's house with its idols and idolatrous priest. Instead of covenant there is ruthless land-grabbing from a peaceful people, blessed by the priest and his idols, and based on the principle that "might makes right." The ultimate irony is that the cult of the golden calf at Dan caused the downfall of the northern kingdom (2 Kgs. 17:16), and Dan became the door for the invading Assyrian forces in the time of the Scribe (Jer. 4:15; 8:16).

The Landless Tribe. As the story of the Danites begins, Dan is landless ("no inheritance," Judg. 18:1). What should have been their inheritance in the southwest (Josh. 19:40-46, 48) was lost to them by the oppression (Heb. *lahats,* Judg. 1:34; see above, pp. 48-49) of the coastal peoples—Amorites or Philistines. Because of this oppression they were embittered, "angry fellows" (18:25; cf. 1 Sam. 30:6, "bitter in soul," translating the same Hebrew expression; Frank Anthony Spina, "The Dan Story Historically Reconsidered," 65-67). As the only tribe without a permanent living place, they were ready to claim religious blessing on their violent appropriation of land for themselves, with no thought of the claims of the occupants.

Land Coveted. The scouting expedition (Judg. 18:2, 14, 17) to evaluate the land to the north and assess their chances of taking it by military force is strongly reminiscent of the same kind of expedition in the wilderness narratives (Num. 13:17-20). The glowing report of the scouts includes words from earlier descriptions of the Promised Land: it was "broad" (Judg. 18:10; cf. Exod. 3:8) and "very fertile" (Judg. 18:9, Heb. *tob;* cf. Deut. 1:25; 4:22, "good"), a gift from God (Judg. 18:10; cf. Josh. 1:3). The expression "no lack of anything that is in the earth" (Judg. 18:10) recalls the similar description of the rich natural resources of the land of Canaan, "a land . . . in which you will lack nothing" (Deut. 8:9).

A closer look at the Hebrew word translated "lack" will show that this description of the land of the people of Laish means not only natural abundance, but also social health due to righteousness in the land. We learn from Proverbs that the causes of "want," or "lack" in the land, are moral: laziness (Prov. 6:9-11), stinginess of the rich toward the needy neighbor (11:24), empty talk without action (14:23), impulsive, ill-considered action (21:5), love of luxury (21:17), oppression of the poor (22:16)—in short, wickedness (13:25).

Nothing in the scouts' report suggests the "wickedness of these nations" which formed the rationale behind God's gift of the land to the Israelites (Deut. 9:4-5). This is no portrayal of "the iniquity of the Amorites" (Gen. 15:16) or of the Canaanite way of death (see above, pp. 15-16). On the contrary, this report of the goodness of the land and the people-land relationship gives the background for understanding the thrice-repeated description of the people of Laish as "quiet and unsuspecting" (Judg. 18:7, 10, 27). This was a peaceful people living in an atmosphere of mutual trust and confidence. Whatever the expression "the manner of the Sidonians" may mean, the fact that they "were far from the Sidonians and had no dealings with any one" (Judg. 18:7) suggests that they were free from the corruptions of Phoenicia (see above, pp. 110-11, and below, p. 157, "Perspectives," no. 5).

In the eyes of the Danites, this "quiet and unsuspecting people" were an easy target and their land a prize for the taking. With the fine words of the scouts in mind, they made off with the idols and the priest who could guarantee the success of their savage attack which wiped out the peaceful people of Laish (see below, p. 157, "Perspectives," no. 6).

Land Lost. The Danites' idolatrous search for land comes to a sorrowful conclusion with the words "until the day of the captivity of the land" (Judg. 18:30). The ultimate result of this kind of conquest without covenant is exile for the people and ruin for the land in 732 B.C.E. The close relationship in v. 30 between the "graven image" which the Danites "set up for themselves" and the "captivity of the land" strongly recalls repeated warnings against worship of strange gods in the good land (Deut. 6:17-19; 11:16-17; Josh. 23:12-13, 16). No such warning is given by the Levite in this narrative, because he plies his trade with the use of idols.

The Danites' idolatry, like the other three idolatries, involved doing "what was right" in their own eyes. The intended blessing of the priest carried meanings which could be understood only in the perspective of history. The Danites' adventure was indeed "under the eye of the LORD" (Judg. 18:6), but it meant not only their own ruin but also that of the entire northern kingdom (see below, p. 158, "Perspectives," no. 7).

PERSPECTIVES

1. The Rebellious, Yet Beloved Son (see above, p. 143)

The ambiguity surrounding Ephraim in Judg. 17–21 is echoed by both Hosea and Jeremiah, where Ephraim is pictured as Yahweh's beloved (Hos. 11:3; Jer. 31:20) yet rebellious (Hos. 12:1; Jer. 31:18) son. The effect on God of the kind of rebellion portrayed in Judg. 17–21 is expressed in the words of these prophets: "How can I give you up, O Ephraim! . . . My heart recoils within me, my compassion grows warm and tender" (Hos. 11:8); "For as often as I speak against him, I do remember him still" (Jer. 31:20).

2. Right in Our Own Eyes (see above, p. 145)

The words "everyone did what was right in his own eyes" may be restated as describing "a normless world . . . a jungle of competing, savage interests." "The Torah," says Walter Brueggemann, "is a line drawn against the darkness and disorder, against the Canaanites and Egyptians, but finally against the chaos and death that waits" (*The Creative Word*, 20-21). Covenant has to do with doing right in the eyes of God. Another has written of the "relativism, nihilism, and cultural despair" of our time, without transcendent values. All goals are thought to be "relative, arbitrary, and changing" (Jeffrey B. Russell, *Mephistopheles: The Devil in the Modern World*, 252).

3. Our History Too! (see above, p. 148)

By baptism Christians are incorporated into the history of Israel, with its saga of liberation, covenant, divine guidance, and the gifts of grace. We should not overlook the story of Micah and the Danites as a part of our own past which we would prefer to forget. In retelling it, we may see images of ourselves. Although we have Jesus as our king (Rev. 17:14) and faithful high priest (Heb. 3:1), we are prone to be deceived by our idols so that our search for legitimate goods (security, prosperity, fulfilling work, living place) becomes destructive of the very goals we seek, at least in the long run.

4. God-Makers Like Micah (see above, p. 150)

Micah was a god-maker and employer of priests. He is a mirror image of those who elevate the products of human effort to the status of gods which they believe to be able to guarantee that their needs will be met. Current examples are economic power, military might (including nuclear power), racial or cultural pride, and political systems.

5. Questions about the Danites (see above, p. 155)

The sensitive reader will ask questions about the morality of the Danites' savage attack which wiped out this peaceful people, and the authority of the scouts' confident assurance that "God has given it [the land] into your hands" (Judg. 18:10). Questions increase when we consider the possibility that the Danites were attacking fellow Israelites living in Laish (Avraham Biran, "Tell Dan," 26-51). In that case they would be guilty of forgetting "the covenant of brotherhood" (Amos 1:9). Once again, we meet the ambiguity, or irony, which the Scribe has structured into his narrative (Norman K. Gottwald, The Hebrew Bible, 260).

6. Laishites and Israelites (see above, p. 155)

Ezekiel described Israel in terms very similar to the Laishites, as "the land of unwalled villages; . . . the quiet people who dwell securely" (Ezek. 38:11). In that scenario, the people of Israel are the intended victims of the armies of Gog, the evil empire (Ezek. 38:2, 12). God comes to the protection of his people in order to set his "glory among the nations" (Ezek. 39:21). No such intervention is recorded for the Laishites. Are we to conclude that what was wrong for Gog was permissible for the Danites?

7. *Modern Land-Grabbers (see above, p. 156)*

We might find in the Danites a mirror image of the Spanish conquerors of Latin America who "totally dislodged the Indian culture by eliminating its leaders, destroying its institutions, and subverting its economic infrastructure." According to José Miguez Bonino this "spiritual 'genocide'" imposed the religion of the conqueror as a permanent sign of defeat. Indeed, religion was "one of the most important instruments of domination" (*Toward a Christian Political Ethic* [Philadelphia: Fortress and London: SCM, 1983], 57). Similar mirror images could be identified in South Africa, North America, the Philippines, Palestine, and elsewhere.

THE SECOND ABOMINATION:
WANTONNESS

Judges 19:1–21:25

DESCENT INTO EVIL

This final episode in the book of Judges marks what the Scribe has presented as the lowest moral point in Israelite history up to that time. In the shocked words of the people, "Such a thing has never happened or been seen from the day that the people of Israel came up out of the land of Egypt until this day" (Judg. 19:30). Ironically, this moral abyss did not come about when the land was being devastated by foreign invasion (cf. 6:5). On the contrary, it was in a time of prosperity resulting from the liberating work of the judges. There was "no lack of anything" (19:19); food and drink were plentiful (vv. 4, 6, 8, 22), and crops bountiful (21:19-20).

The people of Israel condemned the Benjaminites of Gibeah for the brutal gang-rape murder of the woman of Bethlehem. Yet the narrative implicates both the Ephraimite host and the Levite husband. Furthermore, it is the people of Israel themselves who conduct the pitiless crusade to exterminate the Benjaminites as well as the massacre of the population of Jabesh-gilead. They also devise the scheme for the men of Benjamin to steal two hundred young women of Shiloh. The descending spirals of evil suggested in the theological essay (see above, pp. 59-60) reach their lowest point at this climactic end of Judges.

Yet the story of descent into evil (see above, p. 68) is surrounded by mystery and ambiguity. God is silent in the first and third parts of the story. There is no divine intervention to save the girl, as in the case of Lot (Gen. 19:10-11); no divine visitant, as in the case of Gideon (Judg. 6:12) or Samson's mother (13:3). No angel (2:1-5) or prophet (6:7-10) speaks. God does not plead or argue (cf. 10:11-14), nor does God raise up a deliverer (cf. 3:9; see

159

above, pp. 62-63). The words of God to the people of Israel in Gilead seem to come true here: "You have forsaken me and served other gods; therefore I will deliver you no more" (10:13). In Paul's words, "God gave them up to a base mind and to improper conduct" (Rom. 1:28). Israel is on its own with the responsibility of making decisions and living by the consequences. Yet Israel does show a genuine desire to purge the land of evil and turn to God for guidance in extremity. In the end, despite all the bloody excesses, restoration begins and peace comes again for a time. In the midst of this descent, an upward possibility may be discerned. The stage is set for the next actors: Samuel, Saul, and David (see below, p. 173, "Perspectives," no. 1).

THE OUTRAGE (19:1-30)

The Battered Wife

This story begins in the remote hill country of Ephraim with two sojourners—a levitical priest who had no tribal home, and his wife (RSV "concubine") from Bethlehem. In view of the negative picture of the Levite in the previous narrative, the reader is prepared for a similar situation here. The first such negative note occurs when the wife leaves her husband because of an unnamed grievance. In view of his later harsh treatment (19:25), we may suspect domestic violence, in either word or deed. In modern terms we would call her a battered wife.

After four months without her, the repentant husband follows his wife to her father's home, seeking to win her back with tender words (literally, spoken "to her heart," as in the case of Hamor speaking to Dinah [Gen. 34:3] or God speaking tenderly to Israel [Isa. 40:2; Hos. 2:14]). The apparent happy ending to the lovers' quarrel is only the beginning of a tragic tale.

Note on the "Concubine" in This Story

The status of the woman here is not the same as the "concubine" who was a minor wife in a family system which allowed for both wives and concubines (cf. Gen. 22:24; 2 Sam. 5:13; Song of Sol. 6:8). In the absence of any mention of other wives, the terms "husband" (Judg. 19:3), "master" (26, 27), "father-in-law," and "son-in-law" (vv. 4, 5, 7, 9) indicate that this woman is not one among many wives (as in 8:31, the only other use of the Hebrew word translated "concubine" in Judges). It must be a term describing a special status which we cannot now recover (cf. John Gray, *Joshua, Judges, Ruth*, 300, 347). The term "girl" (19:3, 4) indicates that she was a young woman.

A Night's Lodging

Four nights spent in making merry and a fifth begun in joy and continued in terror dominate the first segment of the Scribe's narrative (19:1-26). The Hebrew word *lin*, translated "lodge," "spend the night," or "tarry all night," occurs ten times in ch. 19, once in ch. 20 in the retelling of the story, and only once elsewhere (18:2) in the book of Judges. In this account, the first five times refer to the seductive hospitality of the host in Bethlehem. The last five tell of the vain search for lodging in Jerusalem or Gibeah.

Hospitality in Bethlehem. Four times the man of Judah presses his hospitality on his son-in-law, urging him again and again to spend the night, eat and drink, and make his heart merry (19:5, 6, 7, 9). The carousing and merriment of the two men night after night are ironic in light of the tragedy to follow. The reader is reminded of similar heedless merriment in Noah's generation (Luke 17:26-27), the Israelites at Mt. Sinai (Exod. 32:6, 18-20), and the leading men of Israel who drank wine in bowls but were "not grieved over the ruin of Joseph" (Amos 6:6; cf. Isa. 22:13).

Finally, on the afternoon of the fifth day, after another bout of food and drink (Judg. 19:8), the Levite resolves not to spend another such night (v. 10). It is, ironically, this tardy departure which brings on the "terror of the night" (Ps. 91:5) which lies ahead.

Homeless at Nightfall. In five quick strokes the narrator tells of the rapid approach of darkness and its dangers. As the Levite prepares to leave Bethlehem with his wife and servant, the day is already declining (Judg. 19:8). Evening is near, and the day is almost over (v. 9). By the time they reach Jerusalem, "the day was far spent" (v. 11). At Gibeah, the sun has gone down (v. 14). Without street lights or the protection of an armed escort, they are threatened by "gloom or deep darkness where evildoers may hide themselves" (Job 34:22).

City of Foreigners. After a two-hour journey, the servant suggests that they spend the night in Jerusalem. The Levite, unwilling to risk a night in this "city of foreigners [Heb. *nokri*], who do not belong to the people of Israel" (Judg. 19:12), refuses. Foreigners would not be governed by covenant teachings and could not be trusted. There is a twofold irony in this description of Jerusalem. First, the Scribe has already told us that the Benjaminites and Jebusites lived there side by side (1:21; see above, pp. 28-29). The implication is that the Benjaminites had learned to "do as they do in the land of Canaan" (Lev. 18:3; cf. Ps. 106:35-39). Second, what the Levite feared in the midst of "foreigners" actually did happen in Gibeah "which belongs to Benjamin" (Judg. 19:14). Gibeah of Benjamin was in fact a city where the faithful would feel like "aliens" *(nokri)* and strangers (Ps. 69:8). In the words of Jeremiah describing the Israel of his day, the "choice vine" planted by God became in Gibeah a degenerate "wild" *(nokri)* vine (Jer. 2:21). So the travelers continue their journey in spite of "the terrors of deep darkness" (Job 24:17; see below, p. 174, "Perspectives," no. 2).

No Room in Benjamin. The callous reception given to the Israelite travelers in Benjaminite territory is emphasized by the remaining four occurrences of the Hebrew verb *lin*. The Levite, having rejected the idea of lodging in Jerusalem, decides to look for a place to "spend the night" in Gibeah (Judg. 19:13, 15). A deep sense of foreboding is created by the narrator's terse comment that "no man took them into his house to spend the night" (v. 15), followed by the old man's ominous warning, "Do not spend the night in the square" (v. 20).

The reader will ask, was there no one in Gibeah like Abraham (Gen. 18:1-8) or Lot (19:2-3) to welcome the travelers? Was no one guided by the law of kindness to the Levite or the sojourner (Deut. 26:13)? Was there no thought of God's concern for the poor, the insignificant, and the powerless as shown in the Exodus, which should have made Israelite society an example of God's redemption (cf. J. Gerald Janzen, "The Yoke That Gives Rest," *Interpretation* 413 [1987]: 261)? The only escape from the terror of the night in Gibeah for these vulnerable sojourners is in the home of another sojourner from Ephraim.

The Night of Terror. The night in the home of the elderly Ephraimite in Gibeah begins like the previous four nights with the two men "making their hearts merry" (Judg. 19:22), while the Levite's wife no doubt enjoys conversation with the old man's daughter. The warmth and security of the home is suddenly broken by the shouts of the "base fellows" of Gibeah. It is possible that they are drunk with festival wine like Gaal and his friends in Shechem (9:27) and are seeking to make cruel sport with the stranger who has come to lodge in their midst. These men belong to the "perverse generation" (Deut. 32:20) who were the perennial problem of Israel (see above, p. 59, and below, pp. 174-75, "Perspectives," no. 3).

Note on the Term "Base Fellows"

The RSV term "base fellows" (NEB "worst scoundrels"; NIV "wicked men") is a translation of the Hebrew expression *bene-beliya'al,* literally rendered by the KJV as "sons of Belial." Benedikt Otzen (*TDOT* 2:131-36) has suggested that the term *beliya'al* may refer to the powers of chaos, as in the phrase "torrents of perdition [*beliya'al*]," which pull a good man to his death (2 Sam. 22:5; Ps. 18:4) or a "deadly [*beliya'al*] thing" which attacks a sufferer (Ps. 41:8). *Beliya'al* may then refer to the person or power that is hostile to God and to God's life-supporting order of society. Israelites were warned against "base thoughts" of selfish gain over the poor neighbor (Deut. 15:9). "Base fellows" draw people away from the covenant God (Deut. 13:13). The sons of a great and good man can become "worthless [*beliya'al*] men" who have "no regard for the LORD" (1 Sam. 2:12). A good king will reject "anything that is base [*beliya'al*]" (Ps. 101:3) and deal firmly with "godless [*beliya'al*] men" (2 Sam. 23:6).

Beliya'al is related to the mystery of evil which enters and dominates the human heart, already alluded to in the story of the Flood as the "evil imagination" (Gen. 6:5; 8:21). Many similarities between this story in Judg. 19 and the story of Lot and his two angelic guests in Sodom (Gen. 19:4-9) suggest that the Scribe is reminding the reader that Israel is always in danger of becoming like Sodom (cf. Isa. 1:10; 3:9) and hence liable to a punishment like that of Sodom (cf. Deut. 29:23-24).

The Crime That Polluted the Land

A careful examination of the words used to describe the terrible events at Gibeah will help us understand the nature of the crime as covenant-breaking sexual violence.

Wanton Crime. The most important word is *nebalah,* used four times and translated as "vile thing" (Judg. 19:23-24), "wantonness" (20:6), or "wanton crime" (v. 10). In this chapter, *nebalah* is used in two senses: to describe the *intention* and then the *act* of the mob of men. Their intention is a "vile thing" (19:23-24) because it violates both the law of kindness to the Levite (Deut. 26:13) and the law of doing no wrong to strangers when they sojourn "in your land" (Lev. 19:33). It is also "vile" because they plan to subject the male stranger to the extreme insult and humiliation of sexual assault. Studies show that in other societies this was a common way of treating the stranger, newcomer, or trespasser, as well as prisoners of war. In a patriarchal society, this would be a way of emasculating him (Peter E. Coleman, *Christian Attitudes to Homosexuality,* 34, 54; Kenneth J. Dover, *Greek Homosexuality* [Cambridge, Mass.: Harvard University Press, 1978], 105).

The "wanton crime" which is in fact committed is the gang-rape murder of the Levite's concubine. Neither the host nor the Levite interpret the law of kindness to strangers as referring to female guests who, in a patriarchal society, are considered property of father or husband. The host offers them his own daughter. This would make her a harlot and the land would be "full of wickedness" (Lev. 19:29). For good measure he includes his guest's wife as well. The Levite, embarrassed by his host's offer, "seizes" his wife and forcibly pushes her out to the men (Judg. 19:25), forcing her to be a part of "folly [*nebalah*] in Israel" (Deut. 22:21). Although he later presents this as an emergency measure to save his own life (Judg. 20:5), the narrative implicates him in the crime.

Note on "Nebalah"

This Hebrew word is related to the noun and adjective *nabal,* usually translated as "fool" or "foolish." The meaning is not so much stupidity or clownishness, but rather thoughtless rejection of Covenant Teaching, the opposite of "the fear of the LORD" (Prov. 1:7; cf. Sheldon H. Blank, "Folly," *IDB* 2:304). *Nabal* may also be translated as "impious," describing those who scoff at God (Ps. 74:18, 22). Words used in connection with *nabal* are "perverse," "crooked," and "senseless" (Deut. 32:5-6). The works of the *nabal* are *nebalah:* "iniquity," "ungodliness," lying words about God, and cruelty to the hungry and thirsty (Isa. 32:6). In short, *nebalah* is a violation of the covenant relationship between Israel and Yahweh (Josh. 7:15) in a way suggested by the theological essay (Judg. 2:20).

Nebalah is most often used to describe a particular kind of covenant breaking related to the code of sexual relations. It describes the premarital sexual relations of a bride (Deut. 22:20-21), Shechem's affair with Dinah (Gen. 34:7), Amnon's forcing his half-sister Tamar (2 Sam. 13:12), and the adultery of the two prophets in Babylonia with their neighbors' wives (Jer. 29:23). It is this particular example of covenant breaking that is the subject of this narrative in Judges 19-21.

Ravish. In order to protect his male guest, the host tells the men to "ravish" the two women to their hearts' desire, and the Levite reports that they have done just this (Judg. 19:24; 20:5; cf. 2:18; see above, p. 82). The English verb "ravish" means rape, but it can also carry the sense of ecstasy, as in the adjective "ravishing." The Hebrew verb *'anah* connotes not delight of the male "ravisher" but the forcible subjection of the female who is "ravished," hence the translations "humble" (Gen. 34:2; Ezek. 22:10), "humiliate" (Deut. 21:14), "violate" (Deut. 22:24, 29), and "force" (2 Sam. 13:12, 14, 22, 32). In other contexts the same verb can describe the Philistine determination to "subdue" (Judg. 16:5, 6) and Delilah's action to "torment" Samson (16:19).

Know. Like the men of Sodom (Gen. 19:5), these men first demand to "know" the Levite (Judg. 19:22). In fact, they do "know" the helpless woman (v. 25). The verb "know" may describe the normal sexual relation between husband and wife (1 Sam. 1:19), but the accompanying verb "abused" indicates that sexual assault is intended here. The English verb "abuse" does not express the vulgarity of the Hebrew, which might be better translated as "make sport of" (1 Sam. 31:4) or "busy" oneself with (cf. Ps. 141:4). For perhaps six hours the gang of men assault the helpless victim one by one, over and over again, while the others look on with raucous laughter.

Abomination. This kind of perversion of the God-given sexual drive was not only "wantonness" but "abomination" (Heb. *zimmah*) in Israel (Judg. 20:6). This word appears in the law as "wickedness" to describe violations of the sexual code, such as incest (Lev. 18:17; 20:14; cf. Ezek. 22:11) and abandoning one's daughter to cult prostitution (Lev. 19:29). The word also characterizes the practices of the Canaanite fertility cult. In the days of the Scribe, Jeremiah denounced "your abominations, your adulteries and neighings, your lewd [*zimmah*] harlotries, on the hills in the field" (Jer. 13:27). From Babylon the exiled Ezekiel referred to the "lewdness" (*zimmah*) of Jerusalem as that of an adulterous wife (Ezek. 16:43; cf. 23:35). He used it as a symbol of the broken covenant.

The Dark Morning

In studied contrast to the prologue, where Achsah is seated happily on her donkey as she goes to claim her wedding gift of fields and water springs (Judg. 1:14-15; see above, p. 32), the epilogue pictures the violated, lifeless body of the Levite's concubine draped over his donkey as the Levite escapes from the city of terror (see below, p. 175, "Perspectives," no. 4).

Two possible scenarios help us think about the morning after. In the first, the Levite callously enjoys the evening with his host. After a good night's sleep, he assumes that his wife has breakfasted with the women and goes to rouse her to get on with the journey home. According to the second, the Levite has a sleepless night because of worry and guilt feelings over what he has done to his wife. With the coming of morning he rushes out to find her, and seeing her prostrate, bends over her to "speak kindly" (Judg. 19:3) to her once again. This scenario implies a shock of realization of what he has done to her.

The Scribe leaves such details to the reader's imagination. He does not speculate about the state of the Levite's mind as he makes the sad journey home. The sequel suggests that, horrified at what has happened, he is forming a plan to rouse the whole people to

166

appropriate action to "purge the evil" from their midst (Deut. 13:5).

The Sacrificial Victim

The grisly events in the Levite's house (Judg. 19:29), which seem to the present-day reader like a scene in a horror show, actually portray the ritual dissection of a sacrificial victim. The phrase "took a knife" appears only here and in the story of the near sacrifice of Isaac (Gen. 22:10). The Hebrew verb translated "divided" is a technical term for the ritual cutting up of the sacrificial victim (Exod. 29:17; Lev. 1:6; cf. 1 Kgs. 18:33).

These words are the clue to interpretation. What we find here is a female sacrificial victim (as in Lev. 4:28), slain by the criminal men of Gibeah, now being cut in pieces. Instead of placing the pieces on the altar to be burned as an offering to God (as in Lev. 1:12-13), the Levite as officiating priest "sent her" (Judg. 19:29; 20:6), in the form of her broken body, to all twelve tribes. The ritual uncleanness of the severed limbs of a dead body (cf. Num. 6:9; 19:16) would symbolize the pollution of the entire land, which, if not cleansed away, would bring utter disaster (cf. Lev. 18:28). Like the slain Abel, this nameless woman, though dead, was still speaking (Heb. 11:4) a mighty protest against this wanton crime committed against her and all women.

Israel's first response is deep shock at the low moral state to which the nation has descended. The words "came up out of the land of Egypt" (Judg. 19:30) are a recollection of their deliverance from slavery into freedom (6:8) and the gift of the land (v. 9), as well as the covenant (2:1) in which Yahweh gave them "the statutes and the ordinances" to live by (Deut. 4:1).

The second response is a determination to learn from the event so that, in the words of Deuteronomy, "all Israel shall hear, and fear, and never again do any such wickedness as this among you" (Deut. 13:11). Three steps in the group process are mandated: (1) "consider" the moral and spiritual implications; (2) "take counsel" together to decide on what action is indicated; (3) "speak" out to make the decision known to all Israel so that common action may be taken (Judg. 19:30).

THE BLOODY SEQUEL (20:1-48)

The Assembly at Mizpah (20:1-11)

Unity Restored. The book of Judges has been arranged to show that the assembly at Mizpah marked the renewal of Israel's unity as a people—a unity not seen since "all the people of Israel" sat weeping at Bochim (Judg. 2:4; see above, p. 54). In none of the stories of the judges did the people as a whole act together. The Scribe's repeated use of the words "all" (20:1, 2, 7, 8, 11) and "as one man" (vv. 1, 8, 11) emphasize the first lesson: the sacrifice of one person opens the eyes of the people to moral chaos and imminent ruin of the whole people, and thus breaks down barriers of suspicion, envy, and rivalry to make common action possible.

In the Heat of Anger. This assembly of "free-and-equal males" (see Norman K. Gottwald, *The Tribes of Yahweh,* 242-43) representing the tribes of Israel met in Mizpah, a cultic center in the territory of Benjamin, with the full knowledge of the Benjaminites (v. 3). The purpose of the assembly was to purge the evil from Israel by taking appropriate action against the criminals in Gibeah (v. 13), or at the least the city of Gibeah, in accordance with the law (Deut. 13:12-16). In the heat of anger, however, the assembly took two oaths: to destroy any tribe who did not attend the assembly (Judg. 21:5), and to refuse to give their daughters in marriage to anyone in Benjamin (vv. 1, 7). The effect of the first oath was the complete destruction of Benjamin and its ally, the city of Jabesh in Gilead. The second oath cut off hope for any future generations. Instead of keeping their war aims limited to the offenders, they went on to destroy all towns and all people of Benjamin (20:48), including women and children. Thus the second lesson is this: in the heat of anger and fear, limits to war aims are forgotten (see below, p. 175, "Perspectives," no. 5).

WAR AGAINST BENJAMIN (20:12-48)

Peace Talks Fail

Wishing to cover up this crime, the Benjaminites refused the request of the Israelite embassy to hand over the "base fellows" who had committed the outrage. They saw no need for purging action, no pollution in the "inheritance of Israel" (20:6), and they recognized no right of outsiders to take action against their men. The moment for peace implied in the expression "now therefore" passed when the Benjaminites "would not listen to the voice of their brethren, the people of Israel" (v. 13). They insisted on their own freedom without moral restraints, so that everyone could do "what was right in his own eyes." Each side then went out to mobilize its troops and make ready for war (vv. 14-15).

Defeat and Victory

In what appeared to be a hopeless contest, the twenty-six fighting units (not "thousands"; cf. Robert G. Boling, *Judges,* 285) of angry Benjaminites with their supermarksmen (20:15-16) were outnumbered fifteen to one. Yet the four hundred fighting units of "all Israel" suffered two humiliating defeats with heavy casualties (vv. 21, 25) before the final victory, which destroyed the entire Benjaminite fighting force except for six hundred men (vv. 46-47). These two preliminary defeats in the bitter civil war stand out in contrast with the wars in which God gave immediate victory (see above, p. 86, on Yahweh's decisive role).

Inquiring of God at Bethel

The relationship of God to this war within Israel is the focus of the three episodes in which Israel inquires of God. As at the beginning of the section of the prologue dealing with the northern tribes (1:22; see above, p. 40), so now at the end, the tribes "go up" to Bethel (20:18, 23, 26) in Ephraim. Each episode shows development in their understanding of the war.

Competition: To Us Be the Glory! The first episode is set before the battle (v. 18). The Israelite forces are full of confidence, not to say arrogance, because of their vastly superior forces. Their question is exactly the same as it had been at the beginning (1:1; see above, p. 13), but now it has a different focus: which of the tribes would gain credit and hence preeminence from going first into battle. The reply expected by some might have been "Ephraim first." This would redress the alleged wrongs done to Ephraim by

Gideon (8:1-3) and Jephthah (12:1). As at the beginning, however, the divine preference is for Judah over Ephraim. As there is no further mention of Judah in the narrative, we may see here a veiled pointer to David of Judah, who would defeat the forces of Saul of Gibeah and Benjamin and bring unity to the people in time to come (see above, pp. 22, 35, on "hope from Judah").

Lamentation: What Went Wrong? In the second episode following their stinging defeat (20:23), a chastened Israel has lost its blind trust in superior armaments, as well as its concern over tribal credit for victory. A whole day of lamentation and self-searching precedes the second question about whether to continue the bloody war of brother against brother. The question shows pain brought by war losses, and confusion because God has not given them victory in their "just" cause.

Sacrifice: Open to God. The third and climactic episode after a further defeat (20:26-28) shows a deepening of Israel's relationship with God. This time, in addition to lamentation, the day-long ritual includes fasting as an outward expression of inward humility before God (cf. Isa. 58:3). At the end of the day, two kinds of sacrifices are made by the priest Phinehas.

The burnt offering, totally consumed in the flame on the altar like Gideon's sacrifice (Judg. 6:21; cf. Lev. 1:9), would serve as a confession of, and atonement for, sin (Lev. 1:4; 4:13-21; cf. Num. 8:19; 25:13). It would symbolize dedication of the whole people to God. The peace or fellowship offering included a communion meal in which the flesh of the sacrificial animal would be shared by God and the entire congregation. This offering would affirm solidarity with each other and with God. The mention of the ark of the covenant at Bethel suggests the possibility of a covenant renewal ceremony.

Only after they have humbled themselves, confessed their sins, and opened themselves to God's grace and power does Yahweh promise victory. The promise is fulfilled when "the LORD defeated Benjamin before Israel" (Judg. 20:35). The reader may well ask whether Yahweh's victory allowed the tribes to torch the towns and kill all the inhabitants of Benjamin.

REPAIRING THE DAMAGE (21:1-25)

A Future for Benjamin

Who Is to Blame? Instead of a victory celebration like Miriam's dance by the sea (Exod. 15:20-21), the people of Israel gather for the last time at Bethel and weep bitterly (Judg. 21:2) in a way reminiscent of the weeping at Bochim (2:4; see above, p. 54). They meet not to thank God for victory but to complain that there is "one tribe lacking in Israel" and to ask God, "Why has this come to pass in Israel?" (21:3). The narrator later even suggests that they thought they wanted to repair the "breach in the tribes of Israel" which, in their minds, *God* had made (v. 15)! Comic irony is surely intended here. The narrative has made clear that the Israelites themselves had wiped out the entire tribe of Benjamin by over-zealous hot pursuit of defeated troops (20:46), by fire and slaughter in all the towns of Benjamin (v. 48), and by a rash oath-curse that condemned Benjamin to nonexistence (21:1, 7, 18). The Israelites themselves had wielded the axe that "cut off" (v. 6) their brother tribe from the tree of God's planting (cf. Isa. 5:7; Ps. 80:15; Rom. 11:17-24).

Belated Compassion. The description of the ceremony on the second day at Bethel (Judg. 21:4) reads like a parody of the covenant ceremony at Sinai. Moses too "rose early in the morning . . . built an altar . . . offered burnt offerings and sacrificed peace offerings . . . to the LORD" (Exod. 24:4-5). The difference is that the hands of the warriors who sat at the communion meal are stained with the blood of the very Benjaminites whose absence they mourn! Their belated "compassion for Benjamin their brother" (Judg. 21:6) which follows the ceremony does not move them to repent for their rash oath.

A Way Out. Having killed all the women of Benjamin (21:16) in revenge for the rape-murder of one woman, and having withheld their own daughters by a vindictive curse, they declare an ally of Benjamin, Jabesh-gilead, subject to the solemn ban which means ritual destruction of every inhabitant including "the women and the little ones" (vv. 10-11; see above, p. 33, for the only other occurrence of the word *herem*). The inappropriate use of holy war terminology only emphasizes the savage irony of this further massacre of Israelite women and children, presented as an act of compassion on Benjamin, to undo Israel's own excesses. Indeed, the suggestion has been made that Ephraim's motive in this action may have been revenge for losses suffered from Gilead in the days of Jephthah (12:6; see above, p. 121).

The Breach Repaired (21:13-15; cf. Isa. 58:12)

The renewal of unity at Mizpah was from the start incomplete. The original covenanted unity of the people had been broken by the very outrage that brought them together. It was this ideal of covenant unity that provided the driving force to bring the offending tribe back into the family. Messengers sent to proclaim reconciliation or *shalom* to the six hundred exiles brought them back to their burnt-out ruins to mourn the loss of their kin—children, women, older men. Now, with hope of progeny, they could begin anew.

Violence Once Again (21:16-23a)

The last act of violence in this grotesque comedy takes place in the vineyards of Shiloh at the time of the grape harvest, reminding the reader of a similar festival at Shechem in the days of Abimelech (Judg. 9:27). The verbs used in the narrative speak eloquently of violence done to women. The Benjaminite soldiers "lie in wait" (21:20) like a man intent on raping his neighbor's wife (Job 31:9), like Abimelech's men (Judg. 9:34), like the Philistines (16:2, 9, 12), or like the ambush of the Israelites at Gibeah (20:29).

Each man would "seize" (Heb. *hataph*) a woman (21:21), as a man in ambush seizes the poor (Ps. 10:8-9). They "took" (Judg. 21:23, *gazal*) their prey as the men of Shechem "robbed" travelers in the days of Abimelech (9:25), in violation of God's command (Lev. 19:13). Here the words refer to forcible seizure of women (Gen. 31:31), as one seizes flocks (Job 24:2), water wells (Gen. 21:25), fields (Mic. 2:2), domestic animals (Deut. 28:31), or a house (Job 20:19; see below, pp. 176-77, "Perspectives," no. 6).

Rebuilding the Ruins (21:23b-24; cf. Isa. 58:12)

The twice-repeated "inheritance" (Heb. *nahalah*) in the closing verses of Judges expresses the continuity of the relationship of

172

Israel with the land. The mission of Joshua to "cause this people to inherit the land" (Josh. 1:6) was accomplished temporarily when he dismissed the people "each to his inheritance to take possession of the land" (Judg. 2:6). The meaning of "possess" involves the ordering of life on the land according to God's Covenant Teaching, as faithful tenants of the Owner of the land (E. John Hamlin, *Inheriting the Land,* 5, 9).

However, the outrage at Gibeah polluted the "inheritance of Israel" (20:6). The result in this case was the ruin of Benjamin's inheritance and the destruction of the population, with a small remnant surviving in exile. Benjamin's return from exile and reception into the covenant family made it possible for them to "possess" their "inheritance" again (the Hebrew noun translated "inheritance" in 21:17 more properly means "possession"). Their task now was to rebuild the ruins and settle down in their homes with their new wives to make a new beginning.

Only when the lost brother was restored to his inheritance could the other tribes go to the land of their inheritance again to apply Covenant Teaching to their daily lives as "the people of God" (20:2).

PERSPECTIVES

1. A Contemporary Story (see above, p. 160)

Stories in the Bible relate to other stories and times in a way that makes them eternally contemporary. The Scribe was being very contemporary when he retold the strange and violent story of the gang-rape in Gibeah and placed it at the climactic end of the book of Judges. We should recall the dark times in which he lived. The good King Josiah had died tragically at Megiddo in 609 (2 Kgs. 23:29-30). His son Jehoahaz, proclaimed king by the people (2 Kgs. 23:30), had been deposed by the king of Egypt (v. 33), who put a puppet king, Prince Jehoiakim, on the throne (v. 34). We learn from Jeremiah that corruption had spread like a cancer throughout Jerusalem and Judah. Jeremiah spoke of theft, murder, adultery, and false oath-taking. He said that "wicked men are found among my people" (Jer. 5:26), "lusty stallions, each neighing for his neighbor's wife" (v. 8). He saw about him "violence and destruction . . . sickness and wounds" (6:7).

173

2. A City of Strangers (see above, p. 162)

Jerusalem, which in the eyes of the Levite was a "city of foreigners" (Judg. 19:12), mirrors the Jerusalem described by Isaiah. Isaiah saw people "strike hands with foreigners" in making forbidden covenants, consult "soothsayers like the Philistines," and bow down to idols of silver and gold (Isa. 2:6-8). They could be seduced by the idolatry of political power ("every high tower"), military security ("every fortified wall"), and commercial might ("all the ships of Tarshish"; Isa. 2:14-16). In such a city, anyone faithful to Yahweh would feel like an "alien" and "stranger" among his own people (Ps. 69:8; see above, pp. 28-29, 36-37, for other references to Jerusalem).

Yet Jerusalem was destined to become a place where the "foreigner, who is not of thy people Israel" (1 Kgs. 8:41), would come and pray to the God of Israel because of the strong witness of the people to their God (vv. 42-43). Indeed, it was the vision of the prophets that in Jerusalem all nations would learn God's ways of peace (Isa. 2:2-4; Mic. 4:1-4) and, according to one psalmist, find the true meaning of their nationhood in their rebirth as members of God's family of nations (Ps. 87:4-6).

In the NT, Christians, as citizens of the new Jerusalem, are charged to welcome the stranger as they would welcome Christ himself (Matt. 25:35) and "show hospitality to strangers" (Heb. 13:2; cf. 1 Pet. 4:9). In the words of Paul, they will be "no longer strangers and sojourners, but . . . fellow citizens with the saints and members of the household of God" (Eph. 2:19). The new Jerusalem will become a city of neighbors, not of strangers.

3. Gibeah, a Mirror for Israel (see above, p. 163)

In a way suggestive for our own day, Hosea spoke of the corruption of his time as a return to "the days of Gibeah" (Hos. 9:9). He said further that the sins of Israel had continued "from the days of Gibeah" (Hos. 10:9). The stubborn Benjaminites who "would not listen" to the appeal of their brothers (Judg. 20:13) were like the people of Israel in Isaiah's time, "a rebellious people, lying sons, sons who will not hear the instruction of the LORD" (Isa. 30:9). Jeremiah called the men of Judah "all stubbornly rebellious" (Jer.

6:28); they were not "ashamed when they committed abomination" and "did not know how to blush" (8:12). As Hosea suggested, the almost complete destruction of Benjamin was a warning of what would happen to Israel (cf. Francis I. Andersen and David Noel Freedman, *Hosea*. Anchor Bible [Garden City: Doubleday, 1980], 535).

4. Israel as a Violated Woman (see above, p. 166)

In a picture remarkably like that of the woman of Bethlehem, Jeremiah saw Zion (the people of Israel) as a woman "gasping for breath, stretching out her hands [and crying out], 'Woe is me! I am fainting before murderers'" (Jer. 4:31; see above, p. 38).

Interestingly enough, Athanasius also compared the suffering Church to the Levite's concubine: "In that case it was but a single woman . . . now the whole Church is injured, the priesthood insulted, and worst of all, piety is persecuted by impiety" (*Circular Letter* 1).

5. A Moral Crusade in Perspective (see above, p. 168)

Jewish mystics, called Kabbalists, spoke of the descent into evil that must take place in order to redeem the goodness trapped there. But they warned of the dangers of the mission. According to these mystics, the untrained person can get trapped as well and become evil (Susanna Heschel, "Something Evil in a Profane Place," *Christianity and Crisis* 46 [1986]: 339). As we have seen, the Israelites later regretted the effects of their purge on Benjamin.

Jehu's coup d'état against the house of Ahab "wiped out Baal from Israel" (2 Kgs. 10:28). However, the purge turned into a bloodbath of such huge proportions (2 Kgs. 9–10) that Hosea, a century later, referred to it as "the blood of Jezreel" which had stained Jehu's dynasty with guilt (Hos. 1:4). A modern example of this kind of crusading excess is the ten-year "cultural revolution" (1966-1976) in China. It was aimed at cleansing the nation of the "four olds" (old culture, old customs, old habits, old ways of thinking), but it turned into a puritanical orgy that sanctioned violence in the name of public good, with massive damage to the fragile social web of Chinese society in transition.

6. Women as Victims (see above, p. 172)

Present-day readers will see here a story about women as victims. Here women are not actors, but rather acted upon. They are managed by men, abused at home, used to protect men's lives, raped, murdered, killed, dismembered, captured, and stolen by men. The descent into evil meant violence against women. By contrast, other women in Judges have been actors: Achsah, good daughter and wise wife (Judg. 1:13-15); Deborah, mother and savior of Israel (5:7); Jael, valiant against the tyrant Sisera (5:24-27); Jephthah's daughter, victim of her father's ambition, but making her death a gift of love to him (11:36); and Samson's mother, willing recipient of divine annunciation (13:3, 9). We should not overlook the proud mother of Sisera (5:28); the Philistine Timnite, who betrayed her husband Samson (14:17); or Delilah, who sold him for a bag of silver (16:18-21).

Violence against women is a continuing phenomenon known in every culture and nation. It may be related to values taught by the religions of the world which see women as inferior to, and hence subject to, the authority and power of men. It is possible that the men of Gibeah were influenced by a myth of Baal and Anath in which Baal raped her "77—even 88 times," causing her to complain that he had "raped her with a chisel" (William F. Albright, *Yahweh and the Gods of Canaan*, 128-29).

Sun Ai Park of Korea writes that "the phenomenon of misogyny (hatred or distrust of women) and scapegoating of women in Asia are evident in wife-beating, rape, incestuous rape even of children, prostitution involving women, men and children, female infanticide or foeticide, unpaid or cheap labor, domestic or hospitality workers overseas, mail order brides . . ." ("Asian Women's Experience of Injustice and Reflection," 45). Similar reports come out of shelters for battered women elsewhere. One woman speaks of having been gang-raped countless times, with the attacks being led by her husband (Judy Webb, "Binding Up the Wounds," *Sojourners* 13/10 [1984]: 25-27).

Christians will see in such victims of violence "the least of these" with whom Jesus identified himself (Matt. 25:40, 45). They will work against misuse of the media to teach wrong values about women and against the use of pornography to debase women.

They will be sensitive to the factors of race and economic status that make some more vulnerable than others to sexual violence. They will look at the misuse of military power against women, as in this story, including abuse by those who would show their military prowess by sexually humiliating a passing foreigner (as some of the skilled fighting men of Benjamin [Judg. 20:16] may have done).

CONCLUDING COMMENT (21:25)

The precariousness, violence, ambiguities, and new beginnings of human existence are well expressed in the final remark which matches the beginning of the epilogue (17:6). The cycle of internal corruption—including political Baalism (see above, pp. 101-2)—and external aggression, when everyone does "what is right in his own eyes," followed by new beginnings made possible by divine grace will repeat itself "until he comes to whom it [the scepter] belongs; and to him shall be the obedience of the peoples" (Gen. 49:10).

SELECTED BIBLIOGRAPHY

Books

Boling, Robert G. *Judges*. Anchor Bible 6A (Garden City: Doubleday, 1975).

Brueggemann, Walter. *The Land*. Overtures to Biblical Theology (Philadelphia: Fortress, 1977).

Burney, Charles F. *The Book of Judges*, 2nd ed. (1903; repr. New York: KTAV, 1970).

Crenshaw, James L. *Samson: A Secret Betrayed, A Vow Ignored* (Atlanta: John Knox, 1978).

Ginzberg, Louis. *The Legends of the Jews*, 6 vols. (1909-1938; repr. Philadelphia: Jewish Publication Society, 1968).

Gottwald, Norman K. *The Hebrew Bible: A Socio-Literary Introduction* (Philadelphia: Fortress, 1985).

———. *The Tribes of Yahweh* (Maryknoll, N.Y.: Orbis, 1979).

Gray, John. *Joshua, Judges, Ruth*. New Century Bible Commentary (Grand Rapids: Wm. B. Eerdmans and London: Marshall, Morgan & Scott, 1986).

Halpern, Baruch. *The Emergence of Israel in Canaan*. Society of Biblical Literature Monograph 29 (Chico: Scholars Press, 1983).

Hamlin, E. John. *Inheriting the Land: A Commentary on the Book of Joshua*. International Theological Commentary (Grand Rapids: Wm. B. Eerdmans and Edinburgh: Handsel, 1983).

Moore, George F. *Judges*. International Critical Commentary (Edinburgh: T. & T. Clark and New York: Scribner's, 1910).

Soggin, J. Alberto. *Judges*. Old Testament Library (Philadelphia: Westminster and London: SCM, 1981).

Articles

Biran, Avraham. "Dan (City)," in *Interpreter's Dictionary of the Bible,* Supplement, ed. Keith Crim (Nashville: Abingdon, 1976), 205.

————. "Tell Dan," *Biblical Archaeologist* 37 (1970): 26-51.

Bird, Phyllis A. "Images of Women in the Old Testament," in *Religion and Sexism,* ed. Rosemary Radford Reuther (New York: Simon & Schuster, 1974), 41-48.

Brueggemann, Walter. "Theses on Land in the Bible," in *Erets: Land* (Amesville, Ohio: Coalition for Appalachian Ministry, 1984), 4-13.

Davidson, Edith T. A. "Intricacy, Design, and Cunning in the Book of Judges." Unpublished paper (Oneonta, N.Y., 1983).

Exum, J. Cheryl. "Aspects of Symmetry and Balance in the Samson Saga," *Journal for the Study of the Old Testament* 19 (1981): 2-29.

————. "Deborah," in *Harper's Bible Dictionary,* ed. Paul J. Achtemeier (San Francisco: Harper & Row, 1985), 214.

————. "Promise and Fulfillment: Narrative Art in Judges 13," *Journal of Biblical Literature* 99 (1980): 43-59.

————. "The Theological Dimension of the Samson Saga," *Vetus Testamentum* 33 (1983): 30-45.

Exum, J. Cheryl, and Whedbee, J. William. "Isaac, Samson, and Saul: Reflections on the Comic and Tragic Visions," in *Tragedy and Comedy in the Bible,* ed. Exum. Semeia 32 (Decatur: Scholars Press, 1985), 5-40.

Ginsberg, Harold L.; Sarna, Nahum M.; and Bayer, Bathja. "Jephthah," in *Encyclopedia Judaica* (Jerusalem: Keter and New York: Macmillan, 1971), 9:1341-45.

Gottwald, Norman K. "Early Israel and the Canaanite Socioeconomic System," in *Palestine in Transition,* ed. David Noel Freedman and David F. Graf. The Social World of Biblical Antiquity 2 (Sheffield: Almond Press, 1983), 25-37.

Hamlin, E. John. "Nations," in *Interpreter's Dictionary of the Bible,* ed. George A. Buttrick (Nashville: Abingdon, 1962), 3:520-21.

Malamat, Abraham. "The Egyptian Decline in Canaan and the Sea-Peoples," in *History of the Jewish People,* ed. Benjamin Mazar,

1st ser. (New Brunswick, N.J.: Rutgers University Press and Jerusalem: Jewish History Publications, 1971), 3:23-38.

————. "The Period of the Judges," in *History of the Jewish People* 3:129-63.

Mendenhall, George E. "Tribe," in *Interpreter's Dictionary of the Bible,* Supplement, 919-20.

Meyers, Carol L. "Of Seasons and Soldiers: A Topical Appraisal of the Premonarchic Tribes of Galilee," *Bulletin of the American Schools of Oriental Research* 252 (1983): 47-59.

Myers, Jacob M. "The Book of Judges: Introduction and Exegesis," in *The Interpreter's Bible,* ed. George A. Buttrick (Nashville: Abingdon, 1953), 2:677-826.

Sarna, Nahum M. "Gideon," in *Encyclopedia Judaica* 7:557-60.

Siff, Myra; Rothkoff, Aaron; and Bayer, Bathja. "Samson," in *Encyclopedia Judaica* 14:771-77.

Slotki, Judah J. "Introduction and Commentary to Judges," in *Joshua and Judges.* Soncino Books of the Bible (London: Soncino, 1950).

Spina, Frank Anthony. "The Dan Story Historically Reconsidered," *Journal for the Study of the Old Testament* 1 (1977): 60-71.

Wharton, James A. "The Secret of Yahweh: Story and Affirmation in Judges 13–16," *Interpretation* 27 (1973): 48-66.

Wright, G. Ernest. "Fresh Evidence for the Philistine Story," *Biblical Archaeologist* 29 (1966): 70-86.

Other Works

Aharoni, Yohanan. *The Land of the Bible,* 2nd ed. (Philadelphia: Westminster and London: Burns & Oates, 1979).

Aharoni, Yohanan, and Avi-Yonah, Michael. *The Macmillan Bible Atlas,* rev. ed. (New York: Macmillan, 1968).

Albright, William F. *Yahweh and the Gods of Canaan* (1968; repr. Winona Lake: Eisenbrauns, 1978).

Boling, Robert G. "Levitical History and the Role of Joshua," in *The Word of God Shall Go Forth: Essays in Honor of David Noel Freedman,* ed. Carol L. Meyers and Michael P. O'Connor (Winona Lake: Eisenbrauns, 1983), 241-61.

Brueggemann, Walter. *The Creative Word: Canon as a Model for Biblical Education* (Philadelphia: Fortress, 1982).

Chaney, Marvin L. "Ancient Palestinian Peasant Movements and the Formation of Premonarchic Israel," in *Palestine in Transition*, 39-90.

Chen Min-sheng. "On The Three Kingdoms," in *Excerpts from Three Chinese Classical Novels*, trans. Yang Xianyi and Gladys Yang (Beijing: Panda, 1981), 123-32.

Clements, Ronald E. *Old Testament Theology* (Atlanta: John Knox and London: Marshall, Morgan & Scott, 1978).

Coleman, Peter E. *Christian Attitudes to Homosexuality* (London: SPCK, 1980).

Cross, Frank M. *Canaanite Myth and Hebrew Epic* (Cambridge, Mass.: Harvard University Press, 1973).

Danker, Frederick W. *Multipurpose Tools for Bible Study* (St. Louis: Concordia, 1960).

Hanson, Paul D. "War and Peace in the Hebrew Bible," *Interpretation* 38 (1984): 341-79.

Hobshawm, Eric J. *Bandits* (New York: Delacorte, 1969).

Hvidberg, Flemming F. *Weeping and Laughter in the Old Testament* (Leiden: E. J. Brill and Copenhagen: Arnold Busck, 1962).

Koyama, Kosuke. *Mount Fuji and Mount Sinai* (Maryknoll, N.Y.: Orbis, 1985).

Park, Sun Ai. "Asian Women's Experience of Injustice and Reflection," *In God's Image*, June 1987, 42-50.

Pedersen, Johannes. *Israel, Its Life and Culture*, 4 vols. in 2 (1926-1940; repr. London: Oxford University Press, 1963).

Polzin, Robert M. *Moses and the Deuteronomist* (New York: Seabury, 1980).

Rainey, Anson F. "Compulsory Labor Gangs in Ancient Israel," *Israel Exploration Journal* 20 (1970): 191-202.

Rudolph, Wilhelm. *Jeremia*. Handbuch zum Alten Testament 12 (Tübingen: J. C. B. Mohr, 1968).

Russell, Jeffrey B. *Mephistopheles: The Devil in the Modern World* (Ithaca, N.Y.: Cornell University Press, 1986).

Song, Choan-Seng. *The Compassionate God* (Maryknoll, N.Y.: Orbis, 1982).

Stringfellow, William. *An Ethic for Christians and Other Aliens in a Strange Land* (Waco: Word, 1973).

Trible, Phyllis. *Texts of Terror: Literary-Feminist Readings of Biblical Narrative*. Overtures to Biblical Theology 13 (Philadelphia: Fortress, 1984).

de Vaux, Roland. *Ancient Israel: Its Life and Institutions* (New York: McGraw-Hill and London: Darton, Longman & Todd, 1965).

————. *The Early History of Israel* (Philadelphia: Westminster and London: Darton, Longman & Todd, 1978).

Wink, Walter. *Naming the Powers: The Language of Power in the New Testament* (Philadelphia: Fortress, 1984).

————. *Unmasking the Powers: The Invisible Forces That Determine Human Existence* (Philadelphia: Fortress, 1986).